MCA
Microsoft® Office S
(Office 365 and Offic

Study Guide
Word Associate Exam MO-100

Eric Butow

To my family and friends

Acknowledgments

I have many people to thank, starting with my literary agent, Matt Wagner. He connected me with Sybex to write this book and managed our relationship well. Next, I want to give a shout-out to my excellent production team: Gary Schwartz, Barath Kumar Rajasekaran, Christine O'Connor, and senior acquisitions editor Kenyon Brown.

And, as always, I want to thank my family and friends for their everlasting support. I couldn't write this book without them.

About the Author

Eric Butow is the owner of Butow Communications Group (BCG) in Jackson, California. BCG offers website development, online marketing, and technical writing services. Eric is a native Californian who started working with his friend's Apple II Plus and Radio Shack TRS-80 Model III in 1980 when he lived in Fresno, California. He learned about programming, graphic design, and desktop publishing in the Fresno PC Users Group in his professional career, and when he started BCG in 1994.

 Eric has written 37 other technical books as an author, a coauthor, or in one case, a ghostwriter. Most of Eric's works were written for the general book market, but some were written for specific clients, including HP and F5 Networks. Two of his books have been translated into Chinese and Italian. Eric's most recent books are *Programming Interviews for Dummies* (For Dummies, 2019) with John Sonmez, *Instagram for Dummies* (For Dummies, 2019) with Jenn Herman and Corey Walker, and *Ultimate Guide to Social Media Marketing* (Entrepreneur Press, 2020) with Mike Allton, Jenn Herman, Stephanie Liu, and Amanda Robinson.

Upon his graduation from California State University, Fresno in 1996 with a master's degree in communication, Eric moved to Roseville, California, where he lived for 13 years. Eric continued to build his business and worked as a technical writer for a wide variety of businesses, from startups to large companies, including Intel, Wells Fargo Wachovia, TASQ Technology, Cisco Systems, and Hewlett-Packard. Many of those clients required their technical writers to know Microsoft Word, which Eric has used since the early 1990s. From 1997 to 1999, during his off time, Eric produced 30 issues of *Sacra Blue*, the award-winning monthly magazine of the Sacramento PC Users Group.

When Eric isn't working in (and on) his business or writing books, you can find him enjoying time with friends, walking around the historic Gold Rush town of Jackson, and helping his mother manage her infant and toddler daycare business.

About the Technical Editor

Kristen Merritt is an experienced technical editor who has reviewed books for several publishers, including Wiley and Microsoft Press. Kristen spent 12 years in technical sales, and she is currently employed as a digital marketer.

Contents at a Glance

Contents

Table of Exercises

Introduction

MCA Microsoft Office Specialist (Office 365 and Office 2019) Study Guide: Word Associate Exam MO-100 is written to help you become a Microsoft Certified Office Specialist for Microsoft Word, which is a component of the Microsoft 365 suite of productivity applications to which you can subscribe. You can also use this book with the one-time purchase version of Word, which Microsoft calls Word 2019.

Microsoft 365 allows you to use the different versions of Word on many platforms, including Windows, macOS, iOS, iPadOS, and Android. You can even use the web version of Word on the free online version of Microsoft 365. This book, however, talks about using the most popular version of Word on the most popular operating system, which happens to be Word for Microsoft 365 running on Windows 10.

You may already know about a lot of Word features by working with it, but regardless of whether you use Word for your regular documentation tasks or you're new to the application, you'll learn a lot about the power that Word gives you to create all kinds of documents.

Who Should Read This Book

If you want to prepare to take the Microsoft Word Exam MO-100, which will help you become a certified Word specialist and hopefully increase your stature, marketability, and income, then this is the book for you. Even if you're not going to take the exam but you want to learn how to use Word more effectively, this book will show you how to get the most out of using Word based on features that Microsoft believes are important for you to know.

What You'll Learn from This Book

What you learn in this book adheres to the topics in the Microsoft Word Exam MO-100, because this book is designed to help you learn about the topics in the exam and pass it on the first try.

After you finish reading the book and complete all the exercises, you'll have an in-depth understanding of Word that you can use to become more productive at work and at home (or in your home office).

Hardware and Software Requirements

You should be running a computer with Windows 10 installed, and you should have Word for Microsoft 365 or Word 2019 installed and running before you dive into this book. Either version of Word contains all the features that are documented in this book so that you can pass the exam.

How to Use This Book

Start by taking the Assessment Test after this introduction to see how well you know Word already. Even if you've been using Word for a while, you may be surprised at how much you don't know about it.

Next, read each chapter and go through each of the exercises in the chapter to reinforce the concepts in each section. When you reach the end of the chapter, answer each of the 10 Review Questions to test what you learned. You can check your answers in the appendix at the back of the book.

If you're indeed taking the exam, then there are two other valuable tools that you can use: Flashcards and a Practice Exam. You may remember flashcards from when you were in school, and they're useful when you want to reinforce your knowledge. Use the Flashcards with a friend or relative if you like. (They might appreciate learning about Word, too.) The Practice Exam will help you further hone your ability to answer any question on the real exam with no worries.

How to Contact the Author

You can email the author with your comments or questions at eric@butow.net. You can also visit Eric's website at www.butow.net.

How This Book Is Organized

Chapter 1: Working with Documents   This chapter introduces you to navigating within a document, formatting a document so that it looks the way you want, saving a document, sharing a document, and inspecting a document before you share it so that all of your recipients can read it.

Chapter 2: Inserting and Formatting Text   This chapter follows up by showing you how to add text to a document; format text and paragraphs in your document using

Word tools, including Format Painter and styles; and create and format sections within a document.

Chapter 3: Managing Tables and Lists   This chapter shows you how to use the built-in table tools to create tables of information, convert the table to text (and vice versa), as well as modify the table to look the way that you want. You'll also learn how to create bulleted and numbered lists in your text.

Chapter 4: Building References   This chapter tells you about how to add and format reference elements in a document, including footnotes, endnotes, bibliographies, and citations in those bibliographies, as well as a table of contents.

Chapter 5: Adding and Formatting Graphic Elements   This chapter covers all of the ins and outs of adding various types of graphic elements in a document. Word comes with plenty of stock shapes, pictures, 3D models, and Microsoft's own SmartArt graphics. What's more, you'll learn how to add text boxes that sit outside of the main text in the document, such as for a sidebar.

Chapter 6: Working with Other Users on Your Documents   This chapter wraps up the book with a discussion about how to use the built-in Comments and Track Changes features when you share a document with others. The Comments feature allows you to add comments outside of the main text for easy reading, and the Track Changes feature shows you which one of your reviewers made changes and when.

Interactive Online Learning Environment and TestBank

Learning the material in the *MCA Microsoft Office Specialist (Office 365 and Office 2019) Study Guide: Word Associate Exam MO-100* is an important part of preparing for the Microsoft Word Exam MO-100, but we also provide additional tools to help you study. The online test bank will familiarize you with the types of questions that appear on the certification exam.

The Sample Tests in the TestBank include all the questions in each chapter as well as the questions from the Assessment Test. In addition, there is a Practice Exam containing 50 questions. You can use this test to evaluate your understanding and identify areas that may require additional study.

The Flashcards in the TestBank will push the limits of what you should know for the certification exam. The Flashcards contain 100 questions provided in digital format. Each Flashcard has one question and one correct answer.

The online Glossary is a searchable list of key terms introduced in this Study Guide that you should know for the Word Exam MO-100.

To start using these tools, go to www.wiley.com/go/sybextestprep and register your book to receive your unique PIN. Once you have the PIN, return to www.wiley.com/go/sybextestprep, find your book, and click Register, or log in and follow the link to register a new account or add this book to an existing account.

 Exam objectives are subject to change at any time without prior notice and at Microsoft's sole discretion. Please visit the Exam MO-100: Microsoft Word (Word and Word 2019) website (docs.microsoft.com/en-us/learn/certifications/exams/mo-100) for the most current listing of exam objectives.

Objective Map

Objective	Chapter
Section 1: Manage documents	
1.1 Navigate within documents	1
1.2 Format documents	1, 2
1.3 Save and share documents	1
1.4 Inspect documents for issues	1
Section 2: Insert and format text, paragraphs, and sections	
2.1 Insert text and paragraphs	2, 5
2.2 Format text and paragraphs	2, 3, 4, 5
2.3 Create and configure document sections	2
Section 3: Manage tables and lists	
3.1 Create tables	3
3.2 Modify tables	3
3.3 Create and modify lists	3
Section 4: Create and manage references	
4.1 Create and manage reference elements	4
4.2 Create and manage reference tables	4
Section 5: Insert and format graphic elements	

Assessment Test

1. How big of a table can you create using the Table grid in the Insert menu ribbon?

    A. 12 columns and 10 rows

    B. 10 columns and 8 rows

    C. 10 columns and 10 rows

    D. 12 columns and 12 rows

2. What search option do you use to find all words in a document that start with the same three letters?

    A. Match Suffix

    B. Match Prefix

    C. Use Wildcards

    D. Sounds Like (English)

3. What menu option do you click to create a new comment in a document?

    A. Insert

    B. References

    C. Review

    D. Home

4. What are the three reference elements that you can add to a document?

    A. Citation, source, and bibliography

    B. Caption, table of figures, cross-reference

    C. Footnote, endnote, citation

    D. Table of contents, table of figures, table of authorities

5. You need to have a link on page 30 of your document that goes back to page 1. What menu option do you click on to get there?

    A. Home

    B. References

    C. View

    D. Insert

6. Where can you find pictures to add into a Word document? (Choose all that apply.)

    A. On a drive connected to your computer

    B. On the Internet

    C. Stock images

    D. Office.com

7. When you need to indent a paragraph, where can you do this? (Choose all that apply.)

    A. In the Home menu ribbon

    B. In the Insert menu ribbon

    C. In the Layout menu ribbon

    D. Using the Tab key

8. Your customers want an easy way to see what's in your document and go to a location quickly. How do you do that?

    A. Add links.

    B. Add a bibliography.

    C. Add a table of contents.

    D. Add a bookmark.

9. How can you quickly change the format of selected text?

    A. By using the Insert menu ribbon

    B. By using the Layout menu ribbon

    C. By moving the mouse pointer over the selected text and selecting formatting options from the pop-up menu

    D. By selecting the style in the Home ribbon

10. What do you have to do before you cite a source?

    A. Select the writing style guide to use.

    B. Add a bibliography.

    C. Add the source to the document.

    D. Add a table of contents.

11. How does Word allow you to sort in a table?

    A. By number and date

    B. By text, number, and date

    C. By text and number

    D. Text only

12. You need to send your document to several coworkers for their review. How do you make sure that you see all their additions, changes, and deletions?

    A. Click the Show Comments icon in the Review menu ribbon.

    B. Add a comment at the beginning of the document.

    C. Click Read Mode in the View menu ribbon.

    D. Turn on Track Changes.

13. Your boss wants you to convert a Word document and share it as a PDF file. How can you do that?

    A. Print to a PDF printer.

    B. Use the Send Adobe PDF For Review feature.

    C. Use Adobe Acrobat.

    D. Use the Home menu ribbon.

14. How do you go to each comment in your document? (Choose all that apply.)

    A. By using the View menu ribbon

    B. By using the Review menu ribbon

    C. By scrolling through the document to read them

    D. By using the Find And Replace dialog box

15. Your boss wants you to create a nice-looking organization chart for the company. What do you use to create one in Word?

    A. Pictures

    B. Shapes

    C. SmartArt

    D. Screenshot

16. What are the two types of lists that you can add to a document?

    A. Cardinal and ordinal

    B. Roman and alphabetical

    C. Bulleted and numbered

    D. Symbol and picture

17. How do you select all of the text in a document?

    A. Click the first word in the document and then hold and drag until all of the words are selected.

    B. Press Ctrl+A.

    C. Use the Home menu ribbon.

    D. Use the View menu ribbon.

18. What category of paragraph styles does Word look for when you create a table of contents?

    A. Title

    B. Subtitle

    C. Strong

    D. Heading

19. What WordArt styles can you add to text within a text box? (Choose all that apply.)

    A. Text Fill

    B. Text Direction

C. Text Alignment

D. Text Outline

20. Why would you change a number value in a numbered list?

   A. Word gets confused as you add more entries.

   B. You have one list separated by other text or images.

   C. You need to add a number value manually for each entry in the list.

   D. You can't change a number value in a numbered list.

21. What wrapping style do you use to get an image to sit on a line of text?

   A. Square

   B. Tight

   C. In line with text

   D. Top and bottom

22. How do you check a document so that you can make sure everyone can read it before you share it with others?

   A. Look through the entire document.

   B. Use Find and Replace.

   C. Use the Document Inspector.

   D. Use the spell checker.

23. How do you change the color for each reviewer in a document?

   A. You can't.

   B. Use the Review menu ribbon.

   C. Add different styles with different text colors.

   D. Show all comments.

24. How do you start a new section on a new page?

   A. Add a page break.

   B. Add a continuous page break.

   C. Add an even or odd page break.

   D. Add a next page break.

25. How do you add descriptive information to an image or graphic?

   A. By selecting the appropriate style in the Home menu ribbon

   B. By adding Alt text

   C. By typing the description above or below the text

   D. By using the Insert menu ribbon

Answers to Assessment Test

1. B The Table grid has enough cells for 10 columns and 8 rows. See Chapter 3 for more information.

2. C When you open the Find and Replace box, click More, click Use Wildcards, and then add the asterisk (*) to the end of the search term. See Chapter 2 for more information.

3. C Add a new comment by clicking the New Comment icon in the Review menu ribbon. See Chapter 6 for more information.

4. C You can add a footnote on a page, an endnote at the end of the document, and citations on a page. See Chapter 4 for more information.

5. D Click the Insert menu option, and then click the Link icon in the ribbon. See Chapter 1 for more information.

6. A, C, D Word makes it easy to add pictures from your computer, stock images installed with Word, and images from Office.com. See Chapter 5 for more information.

7. A, C You can add a one-half indent in the Home menu ribbon and add more precise indent spacing in the Layout menu ribbon. See Chapter 2 for more information.

8. C You can create a table of contents (TOC) easily so that readers can get a summary of what's in your document and click the entry they want in the table to go to the section on the appropriate page. See Chapter 4 for more information.

9. C A pop-up menu appears after you move the mouse pointer on the selected text so that you can change the format including the font style, font size, styles, and more. See Chapter 1 for more information.

10. C You need to add the source to a document so that Word can find it and cite it. See Chapter 4 for more information.

11. B You can sort by text, number, and date in a table column. See Chapter 3 for more information.

12. D Track Changes adds information to your document so that you can see the changes that reviewers have made. See Chapter 6 for more information.

13. B Word allows you to convert a Word document after you click File ➢ Share ➢ Send Adobe PDF For Review. See Chapter 1 for more information.

14. B, C You can scroll through the document, or you can click the Previous and Next icons in the Review menu ribbon. See Chapter 6 for more information.

15. C SmartArt is a set of custom diagrams, including organizational charts, which you can add and edit quickly. See Chapter 5 for more information.

16. C You can add bulleted and numbered lists in a variety of styles. See Chapter 3 for more information.

17. B You select all text in a document quickly by pressing Ctrl+A. See Chapter 2 for more information.

18. D Word adds text with Heading styles as entries in a table of contents. See Chapter 4 for more information.

19. A, D Text Fill and Text Outline are two WordArt styles that you can apply. See Chapter 5 for more information.

20. B You may need to have the numbered list continue from the entry in the previous list, or you may need the second numbered list reset to 1. You can do both in Word. See Chapter 3 for more information.

21. C When you wrap an object in line with text, the object is added to the document at the cursor point. See Chapter 5 for more information.

22. C The Document Inspector checks your document to ensure that people of all abilities and Word versions can open and read your document. See Chapter 1 for more information.

23. A Word assigns colors to each reviewer automatically. See Chapter 6 for more information.

24. D A next page break ends the current section and creates a new section on the next page. See Chapter 2 for more information.

25. B Alt text attaches descriptive information that appears when the user moves the mouse over the object. See Chapter 5 for more information.

Chapter

1

Working with Documents

MICROSOFT EXAM OBJECTIVES COVERED IN THIS CHAPTER:

✓ **Manage documents**

- Navigate within documents
  - Search for text
  - Link to locations within documents
  - Move to specific locations and objects in documents
  - Show and hide formatting symbols and hidden text
- Format documents
  - Set up document pages
  - Apply style sets
  - Insert and modify headers and footers
  - Configure page background elements
- Save and share documents
  - Save documents in alternative file formats
  - Modify basic document properties
  - Modify print settings
  - Share documents electronically
- Inspect documents for issues
  - Locate and remove hidden properties and personal information
  - Find and correct accessibility issues
  - Locate and correct compatibility issues

You're reading this book because you want to study for and pass the MO-100 Microsoft Word (Word and Word 2019) exam and become a certified Microsoft Office Specialist: Word Associate. I hope you have your favorite beverage nearby, you're comfortable, and you have Word fired up so that you can go through the exercises in this chapter.

Before embarking on a road trip, we often refer to the directions provided by our favorite map app before we leave. In this chapter, I'll show you how to work with documents, including navigating within documents so that you can edit them easily. Next, I'll show you how to format documents to make them look the way you want.

When you know how to control your documents, I'll show you how to save them in the format you want and share them with other people. Finally, I'll show you how to *inspect* your documents so that you can find and remove hidden properties as well as fix any issues with accessibility and compatibility.

I'll have an exercise at the end of every section within this chapter so that you can practice doing different tasks. Then, at the end of this chapter, you'll find a set of review questions that mimic the test questions you'll see on the MO-100 exam.

Navigating Within Documents

It's easy just to fire up Word and start writing. But, of course, you're doing more than just writing. You inevitably need to start moving around the document and making changes to it, and in this section I talk about the tools Word gives you to do those tasks.

Microsoft has added a lot of powerful *search* features to Word so that you can find the text you're looking for pretty easily. You can access these tools through menu options and their associated ribbons, as well as by using keyboard shortcuts.

If you want to move quickly from one location in a long document to another so that you don't have to keep scrolling up and down a lot of pages, Word makes it easy to add a *link* within your document. You can also use tools in the ribbon, as well as keyboard shortcuts, to go to different spots in your document.

Word also has a lot of hidden formatting symbols that you can show. What's more, you can hide text that you don't want to see cluttering your document, but Word also makes it easy to reveal *hidden text* whenever you want to see it.

Searching for Text

Unless you have only a small amount of text in your document, you'll find that you need help locating the words that you want. Word has you covered with tools not only to find words in your document, but to replace them easily as well.

Using the Search Bar

The Search bar appears within the Word window's title bar to make it more conspicuous. Type one or more search terms in the Search box, and then click the terms within the Find In Document area in the drop-down list. The Navigation pane opens on the left side of the Word window and displays a list of results (see Figure 1.1).

FIGURE 1.1   Navigation pane

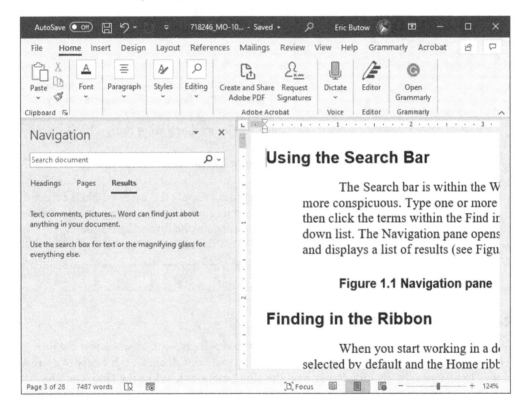

Finding in the Ribbon

When you start working in a document, the Home menu option is selected by default and the Home ribbon appears underneath. Within the Home ribbon, icons appear separated into several sections. On the right side of the ribbon, the Editing section contains the Find icon.

After you click the icon, the Navigation pane appears. Within the pane, type your search term(s) in the Search box and then Word shows you a list of results, as shown in Figure 1.2. Word also takes you to the first instance of the search term(s) in the document itself.

 Microsoft places the titles of each section within a ribbon at the bottom center of the section instead of the top.

FIGURE 1.2   List of search results

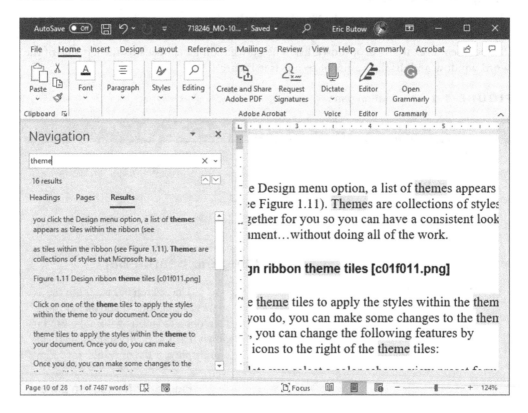

Replacing in the Ribbon

Sometimes, you may want to find a word in order to replace it, such as when you need to replace a product name with an updated one throughout your document. It's easy to do this in the Home screen by clicking Replace on the Home ribbon. Just like the Find icon, the Replace icon appears in the Editing section.

After you click the Replace icon, the Find And Replace dialog box appears with the Replace tab open (see Figure 1.3). This dialog box is probably familiar to you if you've used previous versions of Word because it's been a standard feature (literally) for decades.

Type the existing text you want to find in the Find box. In the Replace box, type the replacement text. Now you can click one of three buttons:

- Click Next to have Word find and highlight the next instance of text in the document.

- Click Replace to have Word replace the next instance of existing text with the replacement text but not replace any other instance. To do that, you need to click the Replace button every time.

- Click Replace All to replace all instances of the existing text in the document with the Replacement text.

FIGURE 1.3   Find And Replace dialog box

 When you click Replace All, Word searches the document after the point where your cursor is located within the document. Once Word reaches the end of the document, a dialog box appears that asks if you want to continue searching from the beginning of the document. If you click Yes, Word continues searching and replaces any other existing text it finds. When Word finishes finding and replacing, a dialog box opens and tells you how many changes it made within the document.

Opening the Navigation Pane

I said earlier in this chapter that you can open the Navigation pane by clicking Find in the Home ribbon. The Navigation pane stays active until you close it by clicking the Close icon in the upper-right corner of the pane.

However, you don't need to click the Find icon in the Home ribbon every time you need to open the Navigation pane. Click the View menu option, and then click the Navigation Pane check box in the View ribbon. It's in the Show section, as you see in Figure 1.4. You can close the pane again whenever you want.

 You may need to click the Show icon in the ribbon and then click the Navigation Pane check box from the drop-down menu if your window is too small for the ribbon to show the check box.

Replacing with the Keyboard

Word has had support for keyboard shortcuts since the first version of Word for Windows was released in 1989. (Windows 2.0 had much better keyboard support than its predecessor, fortunately.)

It's easy to open the Navigation pane using the keyboard—just press Ctrl+F. If you want to open the Find And Replace dialog box, use the same key combination that Word has used for decades: Ctrl+H.

FIGURE 1.4   The Navigation Pane check box

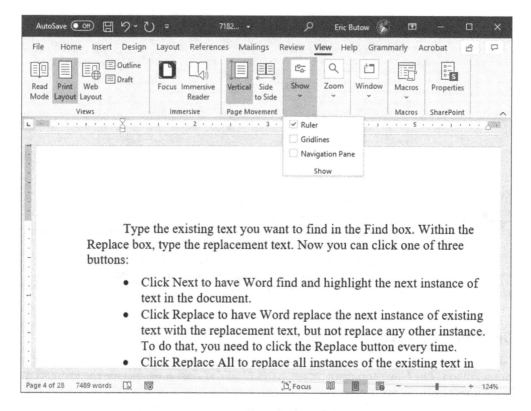

Linking to Locations Within Documents

You can put in a link in one place in your document that links to another place, such as a link on page 27 that will take you to the beginning of the document. Here's how to do it:

1. Click the word in the document that you want to use in the link.

2. Click the Insert menu option.

3. Within the Insert ribbon, click the Link icon.

4. Click Insert Link in the drop-down menu.

5. In the Insert Hyperlink dialog box shown in Figure 1.5, click the Place In This Document option under Link To.

6. Click what you want to link to. From the Select A Place In This Document list box, click Top Of The Document, for example.

7. Click OK.

Now the link appears in your text.

FIGURE 1.5   Hyperlink dialog box

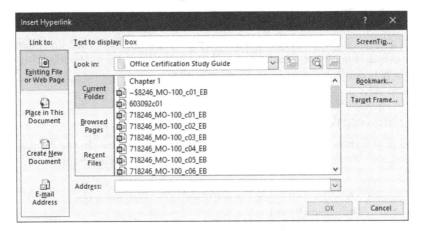

Moving to Specific Locations and Objects in Documents

Word makes it easier (I didn't say easy) to move to a specific location or an object. Start by clicking the Home menu option if it isn't already open.

Within the ribbon, click the down arrow to the right of Find (it's in the Editing section). Click Go To in the drop-down menu.

Now you see the trusty Find And Replace dialog box, but the Go To tab is selected, as shown in Figure 1.6. Scroll up and down in the Go To What list, and then click on what you want to go to. It can be a location, such as a page in your document, or an object, such as a graphic.

What you see next depends on what you select. The default place to go is on a page in your document, so type the page number and then click Next to go to that page. You click an object in the list and then select an object by clicking in the Any Object list to view the list of options. When you click one, click Next to move the cursor to it.

FIGURE 1.6   Go To tab

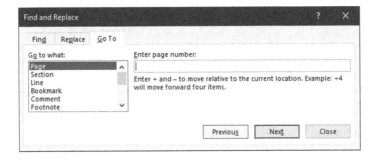

Showing and Hiding Formatting Symbols and Hidden Text

Word adds a bunch of formatting symbols like paragraph marks in your document, but Microsoft is nice enough not to clutter your document with them by default. You can also hide text such as comments within the document that most people who read it in Word don't need to see.

Formatting Symbols

It's easy to view formatting symbols from within the Home ribbon. In the Paragraph section, click the Show/Hide ¶ icon that looks, of course, like a paragraph mark (see Figure 1.7).

FIGURE 1.7   Show/Hide ¶ icon

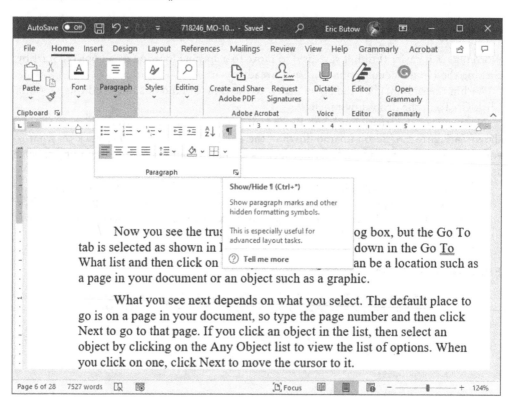

Now you see all the paragraph marks and other symbols, like a square dot that denotes a space. When you're done, click the icon again to turn off the formatting symbols.

If you want to turn formatting symbols on and off more quickly, press Ctrl+Shift+8 on your keyboard.

Hidden Text

You can hide text that you select within the document, and you can even hide text in the entire document.

Selected Text

Here's how to hide selected text (and show it again):

1. Select the text that you want to hide.

2. Right-click in the selection, and then click Font in the pop-up menu or press Ctrl+Shift+F on your keyboard.

3. In the Font dialog box, as shown in Figure 1.8, click the Hidden check box under Effects.

4. Click OK.

FIGURE 1.8   Font dialog box

Now the text is hidden and doesn't show up at all, which leaves you with the potential pitfall of accidentally deleting hidden text. So how do you show the text again?

You'll need to show hidden text for the entire document, as I'll describe in the next section. However, if you know where the hidden text is located, then select the text before and after the hidden text. Now you can repeat steps 2–4 and you'll see your text restored.

For the Entire Document

You can tell Word to hide text for the entire document and yet still view the hidden text (with some formatting). This is especially useful if you've lost track of your hidden text. Here's what to do:

1. Click the File menu option.

2. Click Options at the lower left of the File window.

3. In the Word Options dialog box, as shown in Figure 1.9, click Display in the menu at the left side.

4. Click the Hidden Text check box under "Always show these formatting marks on the screen" to show all text with hidden text formatting.

5. Click OK.

FIGURE 1.9   Word Options dialog box

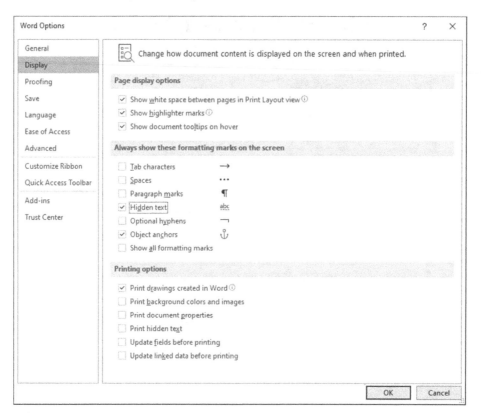

Now all of the hidden text in your document has a dotted black line underneath the hidden characters. If you share the Word document itself, the other person will be able to see the hidden characters. When you save the document to another format (like PDF) or print it, the hidden text doesn't appear.

EXERCISE 1.1

Navigating and Modifying Text in a Document

1. Open an existing Word document, preferably one that has multiple pages.

2. Open the Navigation pane.

3. Search for a word and click one of the results in the list to have Word highlight the result on the page.

4. Replace the word you found by opening the Find And Replace dialog box.

5. Since the word you want to replace is already in the Find box, type the new word in the Replace box.

6. Replace all of the words in the document.

7. Continue by scrolling to the end of the document. An easier way to get to the end is to press Ctrl+End on your keyboard.

8. Add a new link to the bottom of the page that links to the top of the document.

9. Select a sentence within a paragraph and hide it.

10. Unhide the sentence.

Formatting Documents

Word uses a basic template, which Word calls the Normal template, for a new document, which Word calls a blank document. When you create a new document, you can also select from various built-in templates, such as a brochure.

However, if you want to format a document to fit your specific needs, you should start with a blank document and then set up your document pages. In this section, I'll tell you how to set up document pages as well as how to create and apply *styles* to text. Styles are a great way to apply *formatting* quickly to more than one block of text.

You may also want to create headers and footers that run at the top and bottom, respectively, of every page. For example, you can add a page number as a footer if you have a long document. I'll talk about those as well as how to create a *background* on each page, such as adding the word "DRAFT" to a document that you want to make sure your readers understand isn't final yet.

At the end of this section, I'll have an exercise for you so that you can learn for yourself how to use Word's tools to format your documents.

Setting Up Document Pages

When you open a blank document for the first time, document pages have a default size, margins, orientation, columns, and more. If you need to change any of your page settings, start by clicking the Layout menu option.

Now that you see the Layout ribbon, the Page Setup section shown in Figure 1.10 sports seven options that you can click to alter your document layout:

- Margins

- Orientation

- Size

- Columns

- Breaks (including page breaks)

- Line Numbers (which lets you add line numbers to your document)

- Hyphenation

FIGURE 1.10 Page Setup section

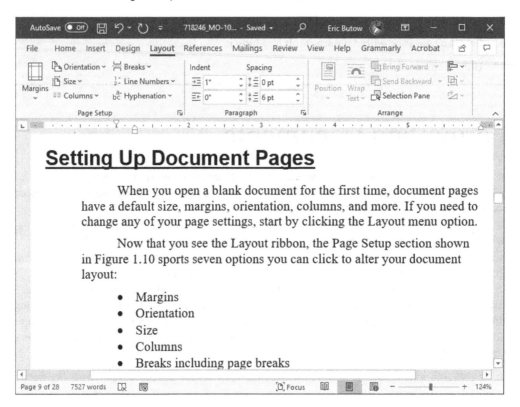

The Paragraph section is to the right of the Page Setup section. Here you can view and change the paragraph indent to the left and right, as well as the spacing before and after each paragraph.

The Arrange section is the last section in the ribbon. Here you can arrange a selected object on the page so that it appears where you want it.

 I'll talk more about page breaks and other formatting tools in Chapter 2, "Inserting and Formatting Text."

Applying Style Settings

Styles are a great way to save formatting information so that you can apply the style to selected text in your document.

When you select text, a pop-up menu appears above the selected text. In this menu, you can apply a style by clicking Styles in the list and then clicking a style tile. Each tile shows you what the text looks like with the style applied.

There are two other ways to find and apply styles: through the Design menu and in the Styles pane.

Design Menu

When you click the Design menu option, a list of themes appears as tiles within the ribbon (see Figure 1.11). Themes are collections of styles that Microsoft has put together for you so that you can have a consistent look and feel within your document. . .without doing all of the work.

Click one of the theme tiles to apply the styles within the theme to your document. Once you do, you can make some changes to the theme within the ribbon. That is, you can change the following features by clicking the icons to the right of the theme tiles:

Colors: This lets you select a color scheme and view preset formats within tiles in different colors.

Fonts: This allows you to select a font style and view preset formats within tiles in different fonts.

Paragraph Spacing: Use this to change paragraph spacing between elements.

Effects: This allows you to change effects for illustrations in your document.

Set As Default: Use this to set your theme or format as the default for all new documents.

FIGURE 1.11 Design ribbon theme tiles

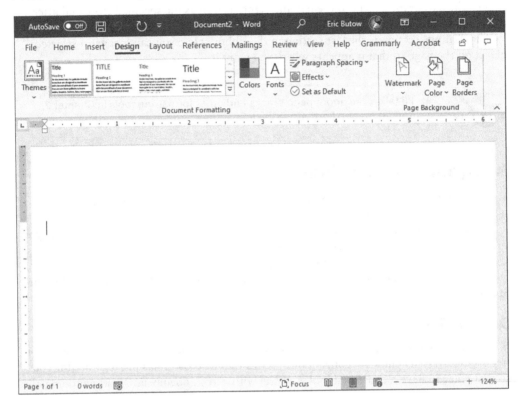

Styles Pane

The catch with using themes is that you have to like the major elements of the theme if you want to use it. A blank document comes with several styles already set up for you, such as heading text.

When you click the Home menu option, open the Styles pane in the ribbon by clicking the down arrow at the bottom right of the Styles area. The Styles list appears, as shown in Figure 1.12, so that you can scroll up and down the list (if needed).

There are two types of styles: paragraph and character. In the list, you see the paragraph mark to the right of the style name. A character style has the lowercase "a" symbol to the right of the name.

Apply the style by clicking the style name in the list. When you click a paragraph style, the style applies to the entire paragraph that you're writing. But when you click a character style, that style only applies either to selected text or to all text you type after you apply the style.

FIGURE 1.12 Styles pane

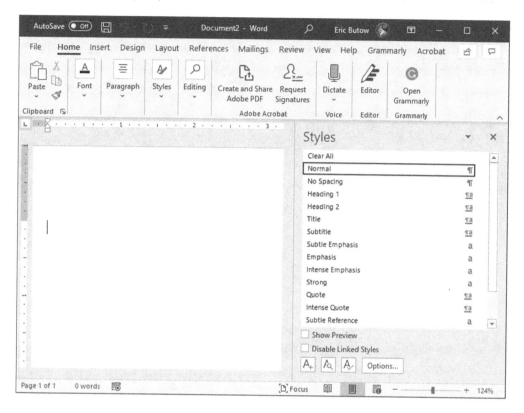

NOTE You can also open the Styles pane using the keyboard by pressing Ctrl+Alt+Shift+S. (You may need to use two hands.)

Inserting and Modifying Headers and Footers

Headers and *footers* can provide consistent information about a document on every page so that you don't need to add it every time. One common way to use a header is as a chapter or section name, and a common footer is (you guessed it) a page number.

You can insert a header or footer by clicking the Insert menu option. The Header & Footer section contains icons for adding a header and footer. When you click the Header or Footer icon, you see the same built-in options in the drop-down menu.

The Header and Footer menus are the same, and so are the design options, though the options look a little different as headers and footers. Figure 1.13 shows the Header & Footer menu.

FIGURE 1.13   Header & Footer menu

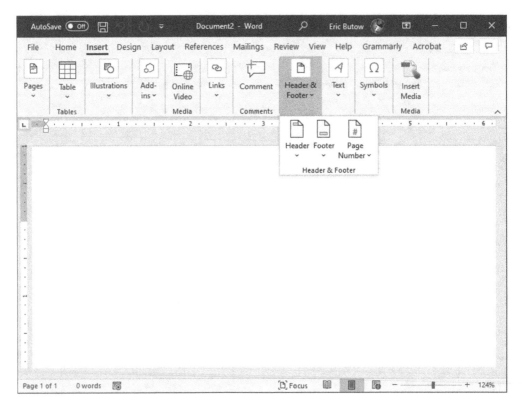

You can also get more header and footer styles from the Office.com website by moving the mouse pointer over either More Headers From Office.com or More Footers From Office.com in the menu and then selecting one of the styles from the submenu if one strikes your fancy.

After you click a design option, the header or footer appears at the top or bottom of the page, respectively. How much editing you can do depends on the option you selected. For example, if you selected the Blank option at the top of the menu, Word puts a placeholder header or footer so that you can edit it to your liking.

Configuring Page Background Elements

A *watermark* is lighter background text that reinforces the document's status to your readers. If you need to add a watermark, such as "DO NOT COPY" or "DRAFT," or you want the page to be a specific color and/or you want a border on the page, Word has you covered.

Start by clicking the Design menu option. At the right side of the Design ribbon, the Page Background section, as shown in Figure 1.14, contains three icons that change the look and feel of your background—and give you plenty of customization options.

Watermark   Click Watermark to add a preselected watermark. You can add your own by clicking Custom Watermark and then adding a picture or text watermark from the Printed Watermark dialog box.

Page Color   Click Page Color to select a color swatch from the Theme Colors drop-down box. You can also select from more colors or set your own by clicking More Colors. What's more, you can add fill effects like a gradient or texture by clicking Fill Effects.

Page Borders   Click Page Borders to set the borders on all pages in the Borders And Shading dialog box. You can select the styles of the borders and where one or more borders appear on the page.

FIGURE 1.14   Page Background section

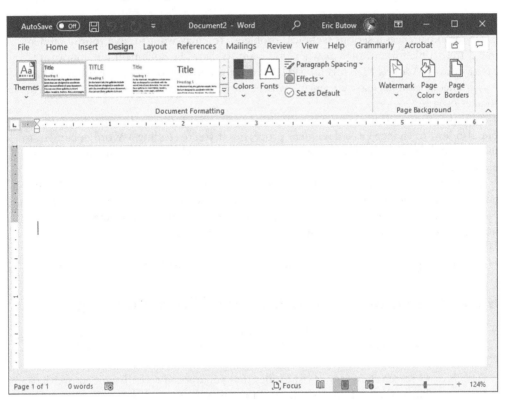

EXERCISE 1.2

Setting Up Your Document

1. Open a new document.

2. Change the margins of a page to the prebuilt Narrow setting.

3. Apply one of the existing themes to your document.

4. Add a header and footer to your document, and add your preferred built-in header and footer style.

5. Add a dark blue background page color from the Page Color drop-down list. After you add it, press Ctrl+Z to return to the default white background.

Saving and Sharing Documents

You should save your document regularly as you work on it in case your computer loses power or experiences a serious technical problem. You may want to save your document in a different file format, such as when you want to share the document but you want to save a copy in Adobe's *PDF format*. (PDF stands for Portable Document Format.) That way, someone can just leave comments within the PDF document using Adobe's free Adobe Reader program.

In this section, I'll show you not only how to save documents in different formats, but also how to change basic document properties if you're sending a Word document to other people and they need to see basic information like who wrote it and any comments about the file.

In case you plan to *print* your document to review and/or share with others, I'll tell you how to modify your print settings, such as how to tell Word what pages you want to print. Next, I'll show you Word's *sharing* tools so that you can send your document to one or more people as an email attachment, in PDF format, as a web page, in a blog, or even as a fax document.

Finally, I'll provide an exercise so that you can practice using these tools yourself.

Saving Documents in Alternative File Formatting

Word can save in any one of 16 file formats, including its native DOCX format. Start by clicking the File menu option and then click Save As in the menu on the left side of the File screen.

The Save As screen shows you a list of files that you opened recently, and above that list you can change the file folder, name, and format. When you click the Word Document (*.docx) box, as shown in Figure 1.15, the list of types appears in the drop-down menu. Once you select one, click Save to the right of the box.

FIGURE 1.15   Save As screen

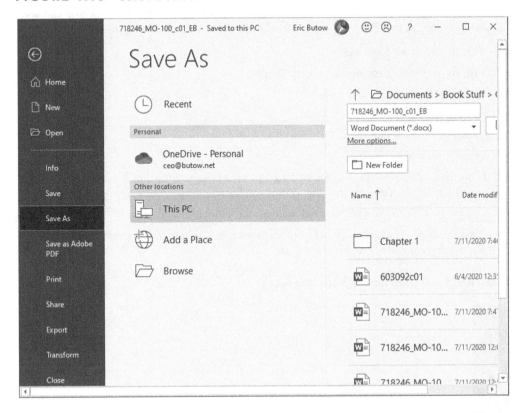

After you save a file, what you see next depends on the format that you selected. For example, if you save to a plain text (.txt) file, you'll see the File Conversion dialog box so that you can tweak the conversion settings. If you save to a Word 97–2003 document, then Word immediately converts the file and shows that older version file in the document window with the words "Compatibility Mode" in the title bar. If you want to continue editing the original file that you created in Word in Office 365 or Word 2019, you need to close the currently open document (your older-version file) and open the original file.

Changing Basic Document Properties

There are standard *properties* and there are those that you can change to help you search for a document in Word and tell people more about the document if they need it.

Start by clicking the File menu option. Now click Info in the menu on the left side of the File screen.

The Info screen contains the Properties area that lists everything you need to know about the document. At the bottom of the list, click Show All Properties. Now you can see all of the properties (see Figure 1.16) and make changes in the following fields:

- Title (if you don't have one)
- Tags to help search for documents in Word
- Comments about the document
- Status of the document
- Categories into which the document falls
- Subject of the document
- *Hyperlink base*, which is the folder path you want to use for all of the hyperlinks that you create in this document
- Company, which is the company that created the document (if any)
- Manager, if there's a manager of your department to whom you report and who is responsible for the document's contents

FIGURE 1.16 Document properties list

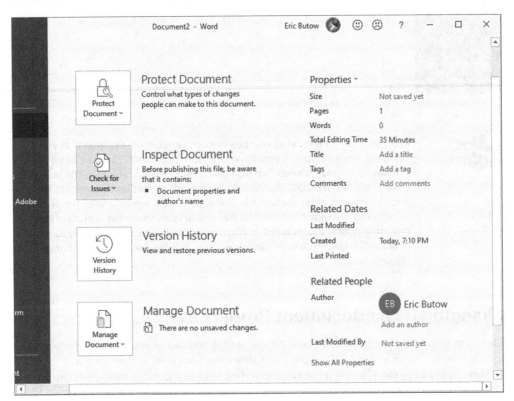

If you don't want to see as many properties the next time you open the Info screen, click Show Fewer Properties at the bottom of the list.

Modifying Print Settings

Word easily detects the default printer that you're using in Windows and lets you change the printer settings so that your document appears on paper the way you want.

Start by clicking the File menu option, and then click Print in the menu on the left side of the File screen. Now you see the Print screen, and the print preview area appears on the right side so that you have a good idea of what the document will look like on the printed page.

Between the menu area on the left and the print preview area, the settings menu you see depends on the printer you have.

In my case, as shown in Figure 1.17, I can change the printer to another one that I have installed in Windows. I can also change different settings for the selected printer, including how many pages to print, the page orientation, and if I should print on one or both sides of the paper.

FIGURE 1.17   Print screen

Sharing Documents Electronically

If you're sharing a document with other people and they expect to receive it in electronic form, such as an email attachment, Word gives you five different ways to send a file online directly within Word.

Start by clicking the File menu option. Now click Share in the menu on the left side of the File screen.

Within the Share screen, as shown in Figure 1.18, the Share With People option is selected in the Share menu. This option allows you to share your document to a OneDrive location by clicking the Save To Cloud button.

FIGURE 1.18   Share screen

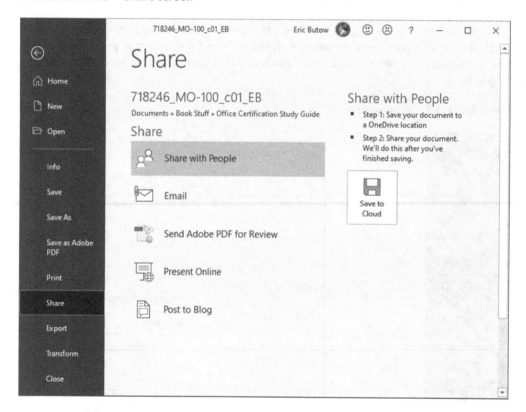

Here are the other four formats that Word supports to share your documents online:

Email   You can send your Word file as an email file attachment in native Word format or as a link to the file in a shared folder on a network. What's more, you can save the file in PDF or XPS format and attach it to an email message. You can even send the file to an online fax service.

If you're scratching your head and wondering what a "fax" is, the word "fax" is short for facsimile. You fax a document by using a device (either a computer or a stand-alone device called a fax machine) to scan the document and then transmit it electronically through telephone lines to your recipient's computer or fax machine. This technology is even older than you think—the first fax machine, called the Electric Printing Telegraph, was invented by Alexander Bain in 1843.

Send Adobe PDF For Review　　Select this option if you only want to send a PDF file as an email attachment, place it on a shared folder, or share it on Acrobat.com.

Present Online　　When you select this option, Word creates a link so that people can read the document on a web page. You need a Microsoft account, which you probably already have, especially if you're using Word as part of Microsoft 365.

Post To Blog　　Word will create a new blog post from your document if your blog is on an intranet SharePoint server or on a public blog website that uses the WordPress, Telligent Community, or Typepad blog platforms. You need to register your blog account with Word the first time you use this feature.

 Real World Scenario

The Case for Sending a Document by Fax

When would you ever use a fax machine? Aren't we in the 21st century? Despite the fact that faxes have mostly been overtaken by email and secure file storage services like Dropbox, you may find in your job that a client in a certain industry requires that you send and receive files through fax. If you work in any of the following industries, don't be surprised if you receive a fax request:

- Health care

- Manufacturing

- Finance

- Government

All these industries have documents with really sensitive information, like medical records, so they require that the documents be sent securely through a fax machine over phone lines or that the sender use secure encryption on online fax services such as eFax, Fax.Plus, and HelloFax.

EXERCISE 1.3

Changing the File Type and Sharing Your Document

1. Open an existing document.

2. Save the file as a plain text (*.txt) document.

3. Close your plain text document, and reopen the Word format document that you opened in step 1.

4. Change your print orientation to landscape, and then print your document.

5. Share your document as an email attachment and send the email to someone else. Just be sure to tell the other person in your email message that this is a test document, unless the document is really something that you need to send to that person.

Inspecting Documents for Issues

If you have any problems with your document, or you just want to take a closer look at it to make sure that other people will (or won't) see the information in your shared document, Word has the tools you need.

I'll start by showing you how you can remove any hidden properties that may be causing problems, such as weird formatting and how to remove any personal information that you don't want to share. I'll also show you how to find and fix issues with document *accessibility* (for people who may have trouble reading your document) and *compatibility* issues with earlier versions of Word.

And as with all previous sections in this chapter, this section concludes with an exercise so that you can get a feel for these tools.

Locating and Removing Hidden Properties and Personal Information

Here's where to find properties and personal information and then use the built-in Document Inspector to remove them.

Start by clicking the File menu option. Click Info in the menu bar on the left side of the File window. Now that you're in the Info screen, click the Check For Issues button. Within the drop-down list, click Inspect Document.

Now you see the Document Inspector dialog box, as shown in Figure 1.19. Scroll up and down in the list of content that Windows will inspect.

FIGURE 1.19 Document Inspector dialog box

By default, the following check boxes next to the content category names are checked:

- Comments, Revisions, And Versions
- Document Properties And Personal Information
- Task Pane Add-Ins
- Embedded Documents
- Macros, Forms, And ActiveX Controls
- Collapsed Headings, which is text collapsed under a heading
- Custom XML Data
- Headers, Footers, And Watermarks
- Invisible Content, which is content that has been formatted as such but does not include objects covered by other objects
- Hidden Text

These check boxes mean that the Document Inspector will check content in all those areas. Click Ink, the only clear check box, if you want to check to see if someone has written in the document with a stylus, such as the Microsoft Surface Pen.

When you decide what you want Word to check out, click Inspect. When Word finishes its inspection, you can review all the results within the dialog box.

The results show all content categories that look good by displaying a green check mark to the left of the category name. If Word finds something that you should look at, you see a red exclamation point to the left of the category. Under the category name, Windows lists everything it found. Remove the offenders from your document by clicking the Remove All button to the right of the category name.

You can reinspect the document as often as you want, until you see all of the categories are okay, by clicking Reinspect. When you're done, click the Close button to return to the Info screen.

Finding and Fixing Accessibility Issues

If you plan to share your document with other users, Word makes it easy to check your document so that everyone of all abilities can not only read your document but edit it as well. Here's how:

1. Open the Info screen as you did in the previous section.

2. Click the Check For Issues button.

3. Click Check Accessibility in the drop-down menu.

The Accessibility panel appears at the right side of the Word window after Word checks your documents (see Figure 1.20). The panel displays your results in the Inspection Results list.

FIGURE 1.20   Accessibility panel

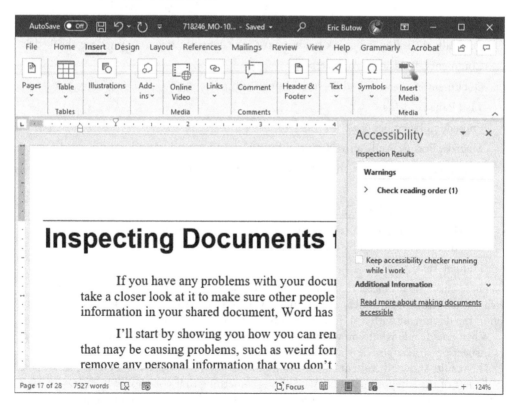

Click the warning to view each issue Word found. Click on the issue to view additional information and steps to fix the problem under the list. You can close the panel by clicking the Close icon in the upper-right corner of the panel.

 You can also open the Accessibility panel in the main document window by clicking the Review menu option and then clicking Check Accessibility in the ribbon.

Locating and Correcting Compatibility Issues

If you're going to share your document with others who use older versions of Word, and you're not sure if what you have in Microsoft 365 or Word 2019 will be readable, Microsoft has you covered.

Start by opening the Info screen as you did in the "Locating and Removing Hidden Properties and Personal Information" section earlier in this chapter. Click the Check For Issues button, and then click Check Compatibility in the drop-down menu.

Now you see the Microsoft Word Compatibility Checker dialog box with a list of any issues Word found in the Summary list (see Figure 1.21). The list includes the number of occurrences of each issue. If there are no issues, Word tells you at the top of the dialog box.

FIGURE 1.21   Microsoft Word Compatibility Checker dialog box

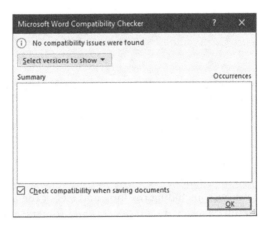

You can check for a specific version of Word someone else is using by clicking the Select Versions To Show button to view a drop-down list of Word versions to check compatibility. You can select from the previous three versions: Word 97–2003, Word 2007, and Word 2010.

What's more, you may find it unlikely that you'll have to open this feature from the Info screen because Word automatically checks compatibility with all three of those earlier versions. If Word finds something, the dialog box opens automatically.

If you don't want to check compatibility when you save a document so that you can check it manually, clear the Check Compatibility When Saving Documents check box.

Unfortunately, you have to remember what the problems are because you can't edit the document while the dialog box is open. Close the dialog box by clicking OK.

EXERCISE 1.4

Checking Out Your Document

1. Open an existing document.

2. Run the Document Inspector.

3. If the Document Inspector finds anything, click the Remove All button in that category.

4. When you're done inspecting your document, click the Close button.

5. Check your document for accessibility issues and make any changes that Word recommends.

6. Check your document for compatibility issues with previous versions of Word.

Summary

This chapter started by exploring the various ways you can navigate around the document to find text that you're looking for. You also learned how to add a link within a document to another place or object in your document. Then you learned how to hide formatting symbols in your document, hide text within your document, and show the hidden text again.

After I discussed how to move around your document, we moved on to learning how to set up your document so that it looks the way you want. Word gives you the power to change many document features, including the look and feel of the page; text setting styles you can apply to a paragraph or selected text; headers and footers; and page background elements, including the page color.

When you finish your document and save it, you can save it in one of 16 different formats in addition to the DOCX format that's native to Word 365 and Word 2019. You can change print settings in Word so that your printed document looks the way you want, and you can take advantage of Word's built-in sharing tools to send your document to others in various formats.

Finally, you learned about the built-in tools that Word gives you to inspect your document before you share it with others. These tools ensure that you don't share any sensitive information, that people of all abilities can read your document, and that people who have older versions of Word can read your document.

Key Terms

accessibility	Inspect
background	Link
compatibility	print
footers	properties
formatting	search
headers	sharing
hidden text	styles

Exam Essentials

Know how to find and link to text and objects as well as replace text in a document.   Understand how to search for text from the Word title bar, the Navigation pane, and the Find And Replace dialog box. Know how to add a link within the document to a different location in the document. You also need to know how to view and hide Word formatting symbols on the page.

Understand how to set up document pages.   Know how to change document page settings from within the Layout tab ribbon. Be able to apply a design template and page background elements.

Know how to apply a style.   Understand how to open the Styles pane and apply one of the built-in styles to a paragraph or selected text in your document.

Know how to add a header and footer.   Understand how to add a header and footer as well as how to select and apply a prebuilt header and footer style.

Understand how to save a document in different formats.   Know when you need to save a document in a different format and what happens after you save the document in a new format.

Be able to change document and print properties.   Understand how to view all of your document properties before you share your document, as well as your printing properties, before you print your document.

Understand how to send documents electronically within Word.   You need to know how to use the built-in sharing tools to share your documents electronically in email and on the web.

Understand how to inspect and fix document issues.   Know how to use the Word Document Inspector to find any potential problems with your documents that you need to fix, including accessibility for all devices and readability for users with older versions of Word.

Review Questions

1. How can you replace text in multiple places within a document most quickly?
   - **A.** Search for the text in the Word title bar and then change each one.
   - **B.** Open the Navigation pane, search for the text, click on each result in the results list, and then change the text for each instance.
   - **C.** Open the Find And Replace dialog box, type the text to find and replace in the Find and Replace fields, and then click the Replace All button.
   - **D.** Scroll down through the document and change any instance of the word that you see.

2. Adding lighter background text to the background of a document is called what?
   - **A.** Header
   - **B.** Watermark
   - **C.** Footer
   - **D.** Style

3. What is the area above the text of a document called?
   - **A.** Footer
   - **B.** Top
   - **C.** Margin
   - **D.** Header

4. Which menu option do you click to inspect documents?
   - **A.** Home
   - **B.** Review
   - **C.** File
   - **D.** Help

5. How do you know a style applies to a paragraph?
   - **A.** The paragraph marker appears to the right of the style name within the Styles pane.
   - **B.** The name of the style
   - **C.** The lowercase "a" appears to the right of the style name in the Styles pane.
   - **D.** The Navigation pane shows that information.

6. What is the difference between a style and a theme?
   - **A.** They're the same thing.
   - **B.** Styles are in the Home ribbon and themes are in the Design ribbon.
   - **C.** The lowercase "a" appears to the right of the style name in the Styles pane.
   - **D.** A style is a collection of formatting settings, and a theme is a collection of styles.

7. Within the File screen, what menu option do you click on the left side of the screen to send a document to someone else?

   A. Info

   B. Share

   C. Save

   D. Export

8. How do you jump to a specific page in a document?

   A. Scroll down to that page.

   B. Search for text you know is on that page within the Navigation pane.

   C. Click the down arrow to the right of the Find icon in the Home ribbon and then click Go To.

   D. Type the page number in the Search box in the Word title bar.

9. How do you find out if a document may be hard for people of different abilities to read?

   A. Send the document to other people and ask if they have any trouble reading it.

   B. Search for accessibility in the Search box within the Word title bar.

   C. Save the document in a different format.

   D. Use the Accessibility Checker.

10. What does the Compatibility Checker answer about your document?

   A. If the document is compatible with the web

   B. If the document can be read in earlier versions of Word

   C. If the document can be exported to other file formats

   D. If you need to use a different word processing program

Chapter

2

Inserting and Formatting Text

MICROSOFT EXAM OBJECTIVES COVERED IN THIS CHAPTER:

✓ **Insert and format text, paragraphs, and sections**

- Insert text and paragraphs
    - Find and replace text
    - Insert symbols and special characters
- Format text and paragraphs
    - Apply text effects
    - Apply formatting by using Format Painter
    - Set line and paragraph spacing and indentation
    - Apply built-in styles to text
    - Clear formatting
- Create and configure document sections
    - Format text in multiple columns
    - Insert page, section, and column breaks
    - Change page setup options for a section

Chapter 1, "Working with Documents," contained high-level information about not only how to add text, but also how to find and replace text in your document. In this chapter, I will take a deeper dive into the various ways of finding and replacing text as well as how to insert special characters.

I will then show you how to format text and paragraphs by using text effects, using the *Format Painter*, and setting spacing and indents for both lines and paragraphs. Next, I will show you how to apply built-in *styles* to text, something I also touched on in Chapter 1, as well as to *clear* any formatting you've made within the text or after you've applied a style that you don't want anymore.

Then I will tell you how to format text in multiple columns as well as add *breaks* to create a new page, *section* of text, or *column*. Finally, I will show you how you can change your page setting options within a section. At the end of each section, I provide an exercise so that you can test yourself and see if you can apply what you've learned.

Adding and Replacing Text

When you open a new document, the cursor is blinking in the upper-left corner of the page. All you have to do to add text is just start typing.

When you need to replace a word, it's easy to replace text just by selecting the word and typing a new one. Yet, as your document grows, you'll find that replacing text this way is too cumbersome, which is why Word comes with a handy find and replace feature.

Finding and Replacing Text

Whenever you need to find text in a document (especially a long document), and possibly replace the text with some new text, Word has this basic function down cold.

Finding Text

There are several ways to find text in your document:

- In the Home ribbon, click Find in the Editing area.
- In the Navigation pane, the last word you entered is the default find term.
- Click in the Search box within the Word title bar, and then type the text that you want to find.

A couple of seconds later, Word lists all instances of the word in the Results list. How Word presents the results depends on the tool you use. For example, when you search for text in the Navigation pane, Word highlights all instances of the text it finds, and it takes you to the first instance of the text in the document (see Figure 2.1).

FIGURE 2.1   First instance of the word "AutoFit" highlighted

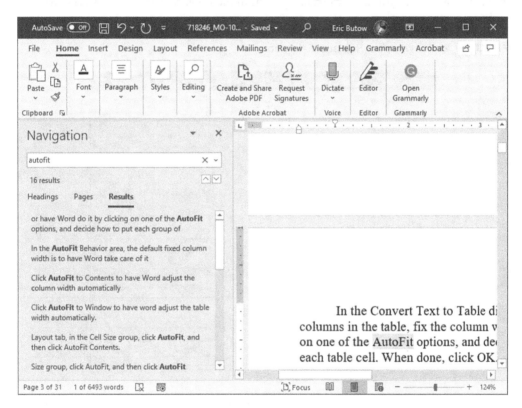

Using Advanced Find to Locate More than Just Text

Change your Find parameters by clicking the down arrow to the right of Find in the Home ribbon and then clicking Advanced Find. The Find And Replace dialog box appears so that you can find using different parameters, including case, the text format, and other *special characters* (such as an em dash) that you'll learn about in the next section.

Replacing Text

When you need to replace text, all you have to do is click the Home menu option (if it isn't selected already). In the Home ribbon, click Replace in the Editing area. The Find And Replace dialog box appears with the Replace tab open, as shown in Figure 2.2.

Replacing text is a two-step process. First, in the Find What text box type the text in the document that you want to replace. Next, in the Replace With text box type the replacement text.

FIGURE 2.2   Find And Replace dialog box

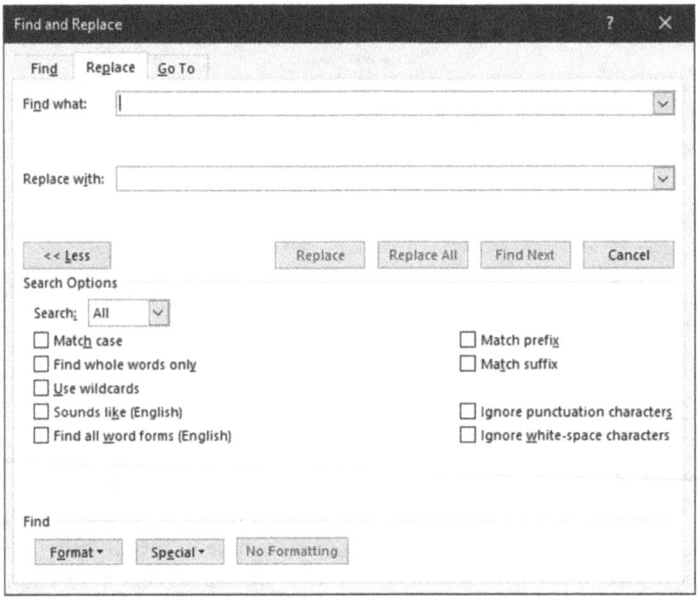

In the dialog box, you see several different options that you can choose to refine your search. When you set one or more options, the options that Word will apply appear underneath the Find text box.

Search   By default, the setting is All, which means that you search through the entire document. Click the All box, and then click Up in the drop-down list to search from your cursor to the beginning of the document or click Down to search from your cursor to the end of the document.

Match Case   Select this check box to find and replace words that match the specific capitalization you've typed in the Find What and Replace With text boxes.

Find Whole Words Only   Use this option to tell Word not to search for matches in a word. For example, if you want to change the word "one" to "four," clicking this check box will ensure that Word doesn't change entries like "anyone" to "anyfour."

Use Wildcards   Select this check box and then type an asterisk at the end of the part of the word that you want to find. For example, when you type **the*** in the Find What box, Word finds all words that start with the letters "the," such as "these" and "theory."

Sounds Like (English)   When you search in the English language, you can find and replace words that sound similar. (Word includes a database that knows what words sound like.) So, when you click this check box and search for the word "there," Word will also find the words "their" and "they're."

Find All Word Forms (English)   Word also has a database of verb tenses, so when you click this check box and search for the verb "wind," Word will also find the words "wound," "winds," and "winding."

Match Prefix   If you have a common prefix in your document, such as "pre," click this check box to find words with the prefix and replace them if you want.

Match Suffix   When you have a common suffix in your document, such as "est," click this check box to find words with that suffix so that you can replace them.

Ignore Punctuation Characters   Use this option to tell Word to ignore any punctuation in the text you're searching for.

Ignore White-Space Characters   Use this option to tell Word to ignore all spaces between characters.

Format Button   Search for and replace existing text or all text that has certain *formatting* attributes such as font types, colors, and paragraph alignment.

Special Button   Find and replace text elements such as a tab or white space. You can also find and replace a graphic in your document with text or a line, column, page, or section break.

No Formatting Button   Click this button to turn off all formatting options you set in the Find What and/or Replace With text boxes.

When you're ready to search for the term or format, click the Find Next button to go to the next instance of the search term.

Click the Replace icon to replace only the next instance of the text with your replacement. If you want to replace any other text that meets your criteria, click the Replace button again to go to the next instance and replace that.

Replace all instances of the text and/or formatting in the Find text box by clicking the Replace All button. If you search from the middle of your document to the end, then when Word finishes its search a dialog box appears and asks if you want to continue searching from the beginning of the document.

When Word completes its search, a dialog box appears in the middle of the screen and tells you how many changes it made. Close the dialog box by clicking OK.

If you just want to find text, click the Find tab in the dialog box.

Inserting Symbols and Special Characters

Sometimes you need to add *symbols* and special characters in a document that aren't keys on your keyboard. For example, you may need to insert the copyright symbol into a copyright statement.

It's easy to insert symbols and other special characters into your text. Start by placing your cursor where you want to insert the symbol and/or special character. Next follow these steps:

1. Click the Insert menu option.

2. In the ribbon, click the Symbol icon in the Symbols area.

3. Click More Symbols in the drop-down menu.

The Symbols dialog box appears and displays 20 common symbols in the drop-down menu. Add one of the symbols to your text by clicking it. If you want to view all the symbols and special characters that you can add, click More Symbols.

The Symbol window appears, as shown in Figure 2.3, and displays many more common symbols on the Symbols tab.

FIGURE 2.3   Symbol window

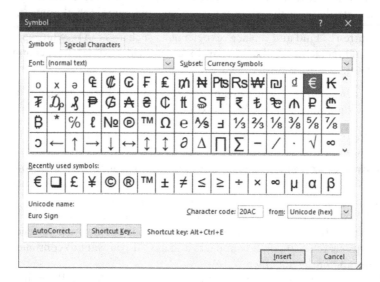

Scroll up and down the list of symbols. When you find the one you want, click it and select Insert.

Different font sets often have different symbols in them. You can change the font by clicking (Normal Text) in the Font box to choose the font set that you want to use from the drop-down list.

You can also choose from font subsets so you don't have to scroll through hundreds of symbols to find the right one. For example, subsets include currency, subscript, and superscript symbols. Click Currency Symbols in the Subset box to view all the subsets in the drop-down list. When you select a subset, the symbols in that subset appear in the dialog box so that you can select one.

Click the AutoCorrect button to add a word or phrase. You can type text within parentheses to insert a symbol or special character automatically. For example, when you type (c), AutoCorrect replaces that text with the © symbol.

Click the Shortcut Key button under the list of symbols to open the Customize Keyboard dialog box and tell Word to add the symbol when you press a combination of keys on your keyboard. Many symbols already have a shortcut key combination assigned to them. If one is assigned, the combination appears to the right of the Shortcut Key button.

Word also allows you to insert a variety of special characters. Click the Special Characters tab to view the list of characters. The list shows you what the character looks like (if applicable), the name of the character, and the corresponding shortcut key.

Click Insert to insert the symbol or special character where your cursor is positioned in the document. The dialog box stays open in the Word window so that you can insert multiple symbols and/or special characters if you want. When you're done, click the Close button.

EXERCISE 2.1

Finding and Replacing Text

1. Open a new document and type several paragraphs of text or open an existing document.

2. Move the cursor to the beginning of your document.

3. Open the Find And Replace dialog box.

4. Enter a word that contains at least one capital letter that you want to replace.

5. Enter the replacement word.

6. Match the case of the word that you want to replace from step 4.

7. Click the Replace All button.

8. Click OK in the dialog box that tells you how many changes Word made.

9. Save and close your document.

Formatting Text and Paragraphs

Word processors have always had the ability to format text and paragraphs from the time Michael Shrayer Software produced the program Electric Pencil in December 1976. As word processors have grown in ability and complexity over the years, especially on Windows and other *graphical user interfaces (GUIs),* you can create and apply all sorts of formatting that conveys the message you want to send in your documents.

Adding Text Effects

Word includes several text effects that not only ensure that your text appears the way you want it to, but that also apply graphical pizzazz to your text to make it stand out. Here's how to apply text effects:

1.   Select the text that you want to change.

2.   In the Home ribbon, click the Text Effects And Typography icon in the Font area.

3.   Click one of the 15 text effects icons shown in Figure 2.4 to apply that effect.

FIGURE 2.4   Text Effects menu

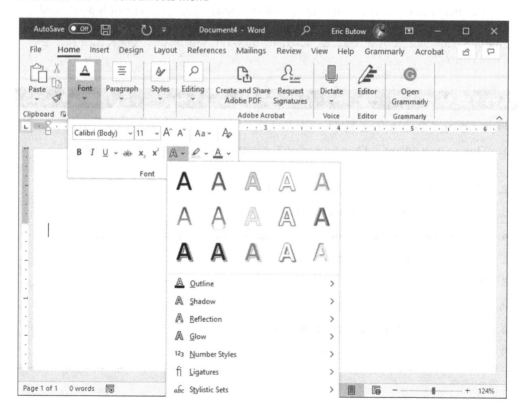

4. Move the mouse pointer over one of the following seven effects to customize each effect in the side menu before you apply them:

Outline: Sets outline colors, weights, and line styles

Shadow: Changes shadow settings

Reflection: Changes settings for a reflection, which is a drop shadow underneath the word that fades from top to bottom

Glow: Sets the glow type, colors, and other options

Number Styles: Sets one of five numbering format styles, such as proportional old-style numbering

Ligatures: Sets the ligature style for your text

Stylistic Sets: Selects one of the built-in style sets that come with your font

Applying Formatting by Using Format Painter

The Format Painter feature is a quick and easy way to apply formatting from selected text or an entire paragraph to another block of text or a paragraph. Follow this process to get started:

1. Select the text or click text in a paragraph that has the formatting you want to copy.
2. Click the Home menu option if it's not selected already.
3. In the Home ribbon, click the Format Painter icon in the Clipboard area, as shown in Figure 2.5.

The mouse pointer changes to a cursor icon combined with a paintbrush. Now you can select a block of text or click inside a paragraph. The text or paragraph that you selected now shows the format you copied.

This process works only once, but you can change the format of multiple blocks of text or paragraphs. After you select the text with the formatting you want to copy, double-click the Format Painter icon in the Home toolbar and then select the text and/or paragraphs. When you're done, press the Esc key.

Setting Line and Paragraph Spacing and Indentation

You may need to change *spacing* between lines and/or paragraphs for readability, or because of requirements from another company or people (like book editors).

FIGURE 2.5 Format Painter icon

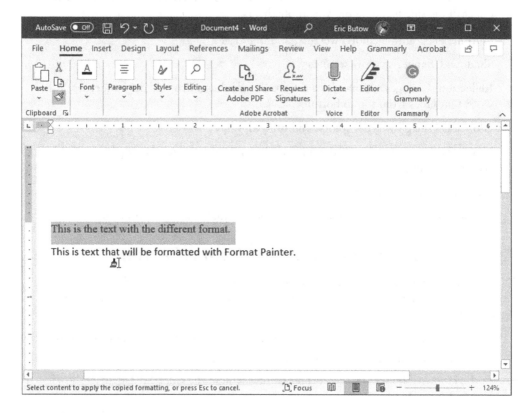

Line Spacing

When you want to set line spacing, place the cursor where you want to start the different line and paragraph spacing, or select the text that will have the different line spacing. In the Home ribbon, click the Line And Paragraph Spacing icon in the Paragraph area.

Now you can select one of the built-in line spacing amounts, as shown in Figure 2.6. For example, clicking 2.0 means that you will see double-spaced lines as you type.

Below the list of built-in line spacing amounts, click Line Spacing Options to open the Paragraph dialog box to set line and paragraph spacing (as well as indents).

Paragraph Spacing

You can change paragraph spacing from the Home and Layout menu ribbons.

> **Home Ribbon** If you want to look at a paragraph's spacing as you make changes, click Add Space Before Paragraph and/or Remove Space After Paragraph in the menu. Word adds a small space above or below so that you can see if you like it.

Layout Ribbon   In the Paragraph area, click the Before or After box to add spacing in points above or below the paragraph, respectively. You can also click the up or down arrow at the right of the boxes to increase or decrease the spacing by 6 points every time you click one of the arrows.

FIGURE 2.6   Line And Paragraph Spacing menu

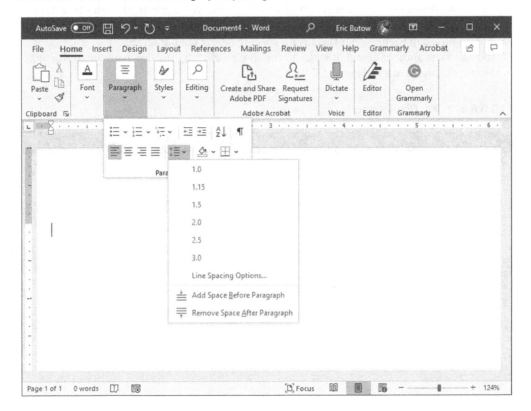

Indenting a Paragraph

When you need to *indent* the first line of a paragraph, you can make changes in the Home and Layout ribbons.

Home Ribbon   Click the Increase Indent icon in the Paragraph area to add a one-half inch indent. Click the Decrease Indent icon to remove the previous indent that you added.

Layout Ribbon   In the Paragraph area, click the Left or Right box to add spacing in points above or below the paragraph, respectively. You can also click the up or down arrow to the right of the boxes to increase or decrease the spacing by one-tenth of an inch every time you click one of the arrows.

Applying Built-In Styles to Text

When you open a new document, Word includes 16 different styles for you to apply to text. You can view and apply these styles to text by clicking the Home menu option if it's not already active.

In the Styles area in the Home ribbon, a row of built-in styles appears with a preview tile. Each tile shows you what the text will look like after you apply it, though some styles may look the same. For example, the Normal and No Spacing styles look the same, but the No Spacing tile can't reflect that there is no spacing below the paragraph.

You can view another group of styles in the row by clicking the down arrow to the right of the last tile, as shown in Figure 2.7.

FIGURE 2.7   Down arrow

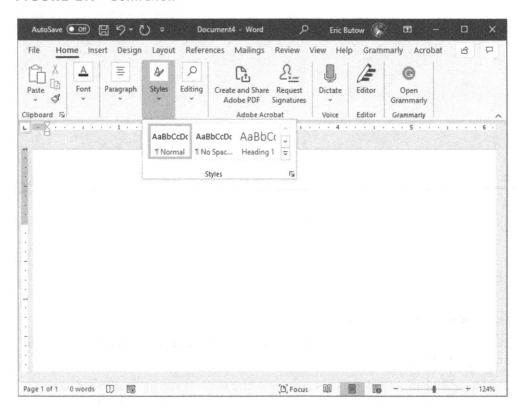

Click the up arrow to return to the previous group of styles. If you prefer to see all the style tiles (see Figure 2.8), click the More button below the down arrow.

FIGURE 2.8   Menu with all style tiles

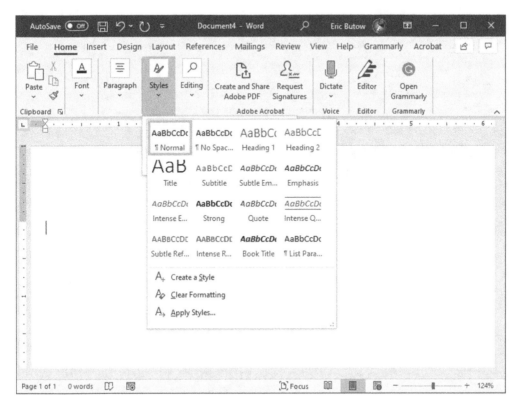

When you select text, you can apply a style from the pop-up menu that appears after you release the mouse button. In the menu, click Styles and then click the style tile in the drop-down list.

    You can view the Styles list pane quickly by pressing Alt+Ctrl+Shift+S on your keyboard. Now you can view all the styles by scrolling up and down the list, if necessary. You can also change settings for a style by right-clicking on a style and clicking Modify in the drop-down menu.

Clearing Formatting

You can clear formatting in selected text or in one or more selected paragraphs.

In the Pop-Up Menu   Start by selecting text in a paragraph, placing your cursor in a paragraph, or selecting one or more paragraphs. In the pop-up menu, click Styles, and then click Clear Formatting in the drop-down menu, as shown in Figure 2.9.

FIGURE 2.9 Clear Formatting option

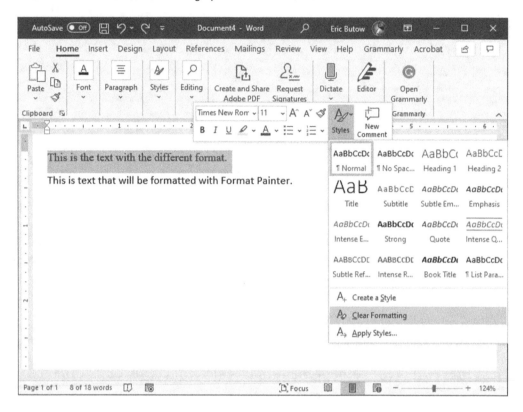

In the Ribbon Click the More icon (a line above a down arrow) to the right of the row of style tiles, and then click Clear Formatting in the drop-down menu (see Figure 2.10).

If you select text in a paragraph, the text reverts to the style of that paragraph. When you select one or more paragraphs, then all the text in those paragraphs revert back to the default Normal paragraph style.

What if you want to clear the formatting of all the text? Press Ctrl+A to select all the text. In this case, you need to right-click on the selected text to see the pop-up menu.

FIGURE 2.10   More icon

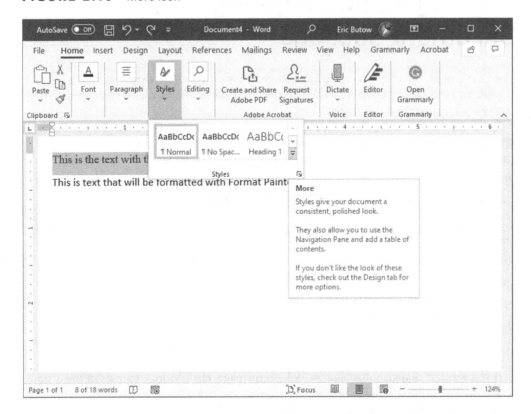

Changing a Paragraph Format

1. Open a new document and type several paragraphs of text or open an existing document.

2. Select a paragraph of text.

3. Apply a blue text effect to the paragraph. (The effect tile is a plain blue A.)

4. Copy the format in the paragraph with the Format Painter and apply it to a word that you want to highlight in another paragraph.

5. Select another paragraph without any formatting and indent the first line.

6. Open the Styles menu and apply the Title style to the paragraph.

7. Clear the formatting in the paragraph.

8. When you're done, save and close the document.

Creating and Configuring Document Sections

Word has a built-in feature to create multiple columns on a page so that your text is easier to read. You can also place columns in a section, and Word allows you to create four different types of sections in a document.

You can have different settings in each section that you create. For example, you can change the columns in different sections. If you create a section on a new page, you can also change the margins, orientation, and size in that section page.

Formatting Text in Multiple Columns

If you want to put your text into more than one column, here are the steps to add multiple columns in Word:

1. Select the text that you want to change. If you want to change all the text, press Ctrl+A.
2. Click the Layout menu option.
3. In the Layout ribbon, click Columns in the Page Setup section.
4. Click the number of columns in the drop-down list. The default is One. You can select as many as Three, shown in Figure 2.11.

If you want to change how columns look on the page, click More Columns in the drop-down list. The Columns dialog box appears so that you can change the number of columns, the width of each column, and the spacing between each column.

 **Real World Scenario**

Creating Different Column Sections on One Page

Your boss has given you the task of creating a one-page marketing document that has one section at the top of the page for an introduction, a middle section for body text, and a third section with a conclusion. The introduction and conclusion sections have one column and the body text section has two.

How do you do this? In Word, the solution is easy. Type all the text that you have in the document. When you're done, select the text that will have more than one column. Now change the column number for the selected text to two.

Only your selected text appears in two columns. The text that you didn't select above and/or below your body text appears in one column. The area with columns may not appear even because you have less text in the second column than the first. In this case, you may have to add a column break, which you will learn about in the next section.

You can add space below the introduction by placing your cursor at the end of the introductory text and then pressing Enter as many times as you need or adding space below the paragraph, a task that you learned about earlier in this chapter. Add space between the body text and conclusion by placing the cursor at the beginning of the conclusion text and then pressing Enter or adding space above the paragraph.

Be careful, though, to keep all your text on one page. As you type in the second column of body text, you see the text that follows pushed down, perhaps to the next page. And as you type text in the introduction, then the body text and conclusion will be pushed farther down on the page.

FIGURE 2.11   Columns menu

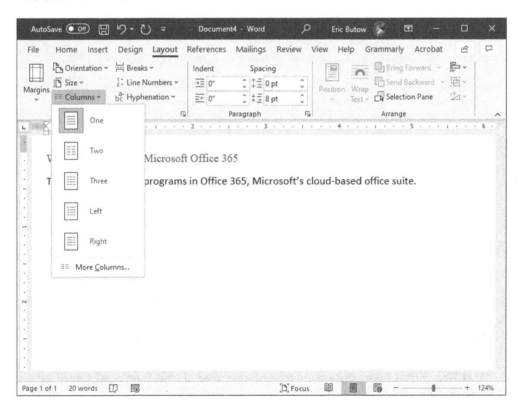

Inserting Page, Section, and Column Breaks

Word makes it easy to insert the page, section, or column break you need. Start by clicking the cursor at the place in your document where you want to add the break. In the Layout ribbon, click the Breaks icon in the Page Setup area, as shown in Figure 2.12.

FIGURE 2.12   Breaks icon

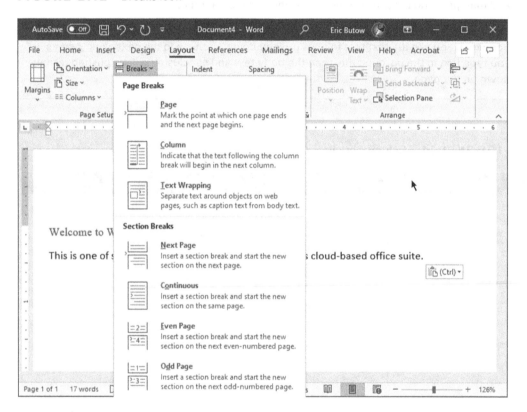

In the drop-down menu, click one of the following options:

Page: Use this option to leave the rest of the current page blank and enter new text on the next page.

Column: Select this option to have text following the current column continue in the next column.

Text Wrapping: Choose this option to wrap text around objects on a page, such as body text around a picture and its associated caption.

Next Page: Use this option to end the current section and create a new section on the next page.

Continuous: Select this option to end the current section and create a new section on the same page.

Even Page: Choose this option to end the current section and create a new section on an even-numbered page. For example, if you're on page 2 and you create a new even-numbered page section, then the next page will have the page number 4.

Odd Page: Use this option to end the current section and create a new section on an odd-numbered page. For example, if you're on page 1 and you create a new odd-numbered page section, then the next page will have the page number 3.

Changing Page Setting Options for a Section

When you add a section on a new page, you can change the page settings only in that section. So, you can have a document that includes one page in portrait orientation with one column and another page in landscape orientation with three columns.

After you create a new page section, your cursor appears on the new page. Now follow these steps to change the page settings:

1. Click the Layout menu option if it isn't open already.

2. In the Layout ribbon, click Margins in the Page Setup section (see Figure 2.13), and then click one of the default margin types in the drop-down menu. If you want a custom margin setting, click Custom Margins at the bottom of the menu.

FIGURE 2.13 Page Setup options

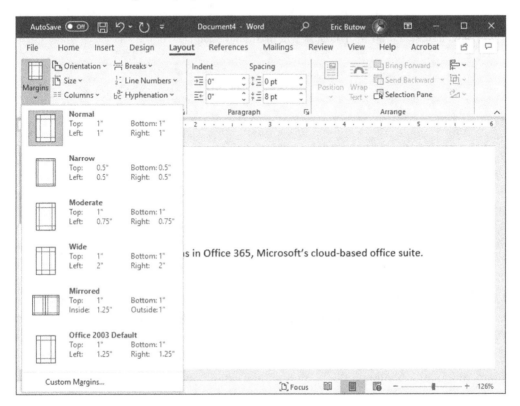

3. Click Orientation to select between Portrait and Landscape page orientation for all the text in the section.

4. Change the number of columns in the section by clicking Columns and then selecting the number of columns, as you learned to do earlier in this chapter.

5. Add page numbering by clicking the Insert menu option.

6. In the Insert ribbon, click Page Number in the Header & Footer section.

7. In the drop-down menu, as shown in Figure 2.14, move the mouse pointer over the position of the page number in the menu and then select the page number style in the side menu.

FIGURE 2.14   Page Number menu

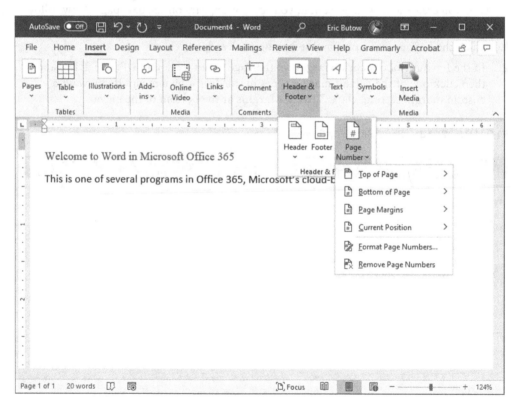

8. Add a border to the page containing your section by clicking the Design menu option.

9. In the Design ribbon, click Page Borders in the Page Background area.

10. Create the border in the Borders And Shading dialog box (see Figure 2.15); when you finish, click OK.

FIGURE 2.15   Borders And Shading dialog box

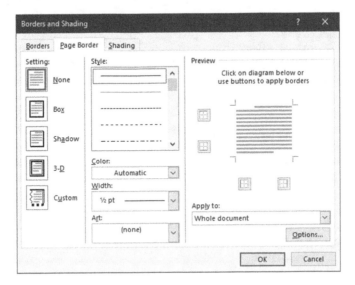

11. Add a header or footer by clicking the Insert menu option.

12. In the ribbon, click Header or Footer in the Header & Footer area. Select the built-in style for the header or footer in the drop-down menu.

After you click a header or footer, the page that has your section displays the header and/or footer. Figure 2.16 shows one of the built-in footer styles.

EXERCISE 2.3

Inserting Sections

1. Open a new document and type some text or open an existing document.

2. Add a next page section break at the end of your document.

3. In your new section, create two columns.

4. Open the Borders And Shading dialog box, select the Box border type, and then click OK.

5. Create a new header and footer, both with the built-in Facet style.

6. When you're done, save and close your document.

FIGURE 2.16 Built-in footer style

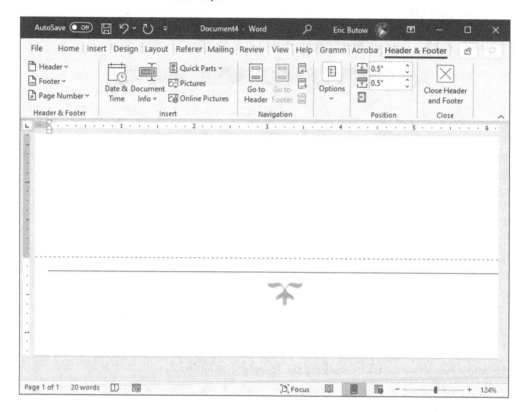

Summary

In Chapter 1, I talked about finding and replacing text, and I started this chapter by going into greater detail. I followed up by showing you how to insert one or more symbols or special characters into your documents.

Next, you learned about how to format text and paragraphs using built-in effects, as well as applying formats using Format Painter. Then I dove deeper into line and paragraph spacing as well as indentation that followed up on what I discussed in Chapter 1.

You also learned more about applying styles that Word provides automatically in new documents, which build on what I discussed in Chapter 1. I finished that section by telling you how to clear all your formatting and start fresh without losing your text (and your time).

Finally, you learned about how to create and configure breaks and sections in a document. I talked a little bit about these in Chapter 1. In this chapter, however, you learned much more, including changing page settings in a section.

Key Terms

break	indent
Clear	Section
Column	Spacing
Format Painter	special characters
formatting	Styles
graphical user interfaces (GUIs)	symbols

Exam Essentials

Understand how to find and replace text in a document.   Know the different ways to find text, how to find and replace text, and how to customize your search by setting different search and formatting options.

Understand how to add one or more symbols and special characters.   Know how to add symbols and special characters that aren't on the keyboard and how to add symbols or special effects by creating a shortcut key.

Understand how to add text effects.   Understand how to access the Text Effects And Typography area to select a preexisting effect and create your own effects in the Text Effects And Typography menu.

Know how to apply formatting using Format Painter.   Understand how to use the Format Painter feature to copy and apply formatting from one paragraph to another in a document.

Be able to change spacing between lines, as well as change paragraph spacing and indentation.   Know how to change spacing between lines and between paragraphs and how to indent a line and remove an indent in a paragraph.

Know how to apply styles to, and clear styles from, document text.   Understand how to apply styles in your document to selected text, as well as a paragraph, and how to clear all formatting.

Understand how to add breaks for pages, sections, and columns.   Know what the differences are between pages, sections, and columns and how to add breaks to change your document layout between all three layout types.

Understand how to change page settings in a section.   Know how to change section page settings, including margins, borders, headers, and footers.

Review Questions

1. When you want to find something in your document using the Find feature, how do you change the find parameters?

    A. The options are available in the Navigation pane.

    B. Click the Find icon in the Home ribbon.

    C. Click the down arrow to the right of the Find icon in the Home ribbon and then click Advanced Find.

    D. Use the Search box in the Word title bar.

2. How do you find and replace words that match only specific capitalization?

    A. You can do this in the Navigation pane.

    B. Open the Find And Replace dialog box and then click the Match Case check box.

    C. Click Find in the Home ribbon.

    D. Scroll through the document and make the changes manually.

3. How do you add a special character?

    A. From the Home ribbon

    B. By selecting the correct font from the fonts list in the Home ribbon

    C. By searching for the special character in the Navigation pane

    D. From in the Symbol window

4. How do you apply a format from one selected block of text to another block?

    A. By clicking the Format Painter icon in the Home ribbon and selecting the other block

    B. Seeing what style the block of text has in the Home ribbon or Styles text

    C. By searching for the special character in the Navigation pane

    D. From the Symbol window

5. How do you apply the formatting from one selected block of text to multiple blocks of text in your document?

    A. See what style is applied to the text, and then apply the style to other types of text.

    B. Scroll through the document manually, select the text, and apply the style that looks like the right one from in the Home ribbon.

    C. Double-click Format Painter in the Home ribbon, and then select each block of text to apply the formatting.

    D. Select each block of text and then apply font and paragraph changes by clicking the appropriate icons in the Home ribbon.

6. How many columns can you add in a document within the Columns drop-down menu?

    A. One

    B. Two

    C. As many as you want

    D. Three

7. What happens when you click the Increase Indent icon in the Home ribbon?

    A. The Paragraph dialog box opens so that you can set the indent.

    B. The first line of the paragraph is moved to the right by a half-inch.

    C. Word highlights the ruler below the ribbon so that you can set the indent.

    D. The paragraph is right-indented.

8. What happens when you add a page break?

    A. A new page opens, and your cursor appears at the top of the page so that you can start typing.

    B. You're still on the same page where the break is located, so you can't see the new page that opened after this one.

    C. A new document opens.

    D. The Page Setup dialog box opens.

9. How do you put a break in one column so that you can continue working in the next column?

    A. In the Layout ribbon, click Columns and then add a column by clicking One in the drop-down menu.

    B. In the Insert ribbon, click Page Break.

    C. In the Layout ribbon, click Breaks and then click Column in the drop-down menu.

    D. Press the Tab key to create a new column and start typing in it.

10. What is a section?

    A. A page

    B. An area in the document that contains its own formatting

    C. It's related to a header and footer.

    D. It's a feature that lets you create an odd or even page.

Chapter 3

Managing Tables and Lists

MICROSOFT EXAM OBJECTIVES COVERED IN THIS CHAPTER:

✓ **Manage tables and lists**

- Create tables
    - Convert text to tables
    - Convert tables to text
    - Create tables by specifying rows and columns
- Modify tables
    - Sort table data
    - Configure cell margins and spacing
    - Merge and split cells
    - Resize tables, rows, and columns
    - Split tables
    - Configure a repeating row header
- Create and modify lists
    - Format paragraphs as numbered and bulleted lists
    - Change bullet characters and number formats
    - Define custom bullet characters and number formats
    - Increase and decrease list levels
    - Restart and continue list numbering
    - Set starting number values

Tables and lists are great ways to present information in your document in a way that's easy for readers to digest. In this chapter, I start by showing you how to create tables. This includes changing existing text to tables, switching tables to text, and creating a table from scratch.

Next, I talk about how to modify tables after you've created them so that they look the way you want them to appear. You'll learn how to sort table data, manipulate the sizes of *cells* and tables, split cells and tables, and create a row header at the top of your table so that the header in your table appears on every page where the table resides.

Then I will show you how to create and format text lists. Word allows you to create bulleted and numbered lists easily, and you'll learn how to add and modify them. Finally, you'll learn how to change number values and *list levels* so that you can manage changes in your lists more easily.

Creating Tables

Word makes it easy for you to create a table. Here's how:

1. Place the cursor within the page where you want to add a table.
2. Click the Insert menu option.
3. Click the Table icon.
4. Move your mouse pointer over the grid in the drop-down menu. Cells in the grid light up as you move the pointer so that you can see the size of the table in terms of *rows* and *columns*.
5. When the table is the size you want, click the highlighted cell, as shown in Figure 3.1.

Et voilà—the table appears on the page with the number of rows and columns you selected in the grid.

FIGURE 3.1   The selected table cells

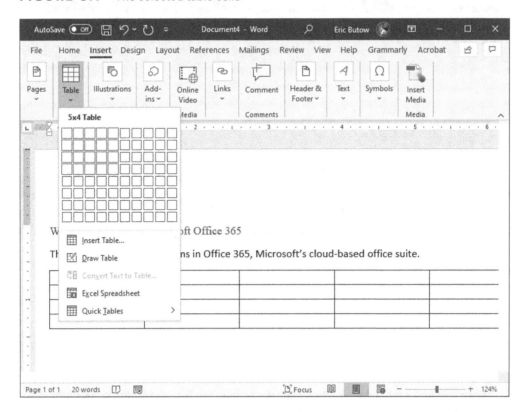

Real World Scenario

Create Tables Quick!

Your boss comes to you first thing in the morning and tells you to put together a document for a sales meeting with a big client in two hours. Word has you covered. Here's what to do to add some nice-looking tables to your document in a jiffy:

1. Place your cursor where you want to add the table on the page.

2. Click the Insert menu option.

3. In the Insert ribbon, click the Table icon.

4. In the drop-down menu, move the mouse pointer over Quick Tables.

5. In the side menu containing built-in tables, as shown here, scroll up and down the list of built-in table styles.

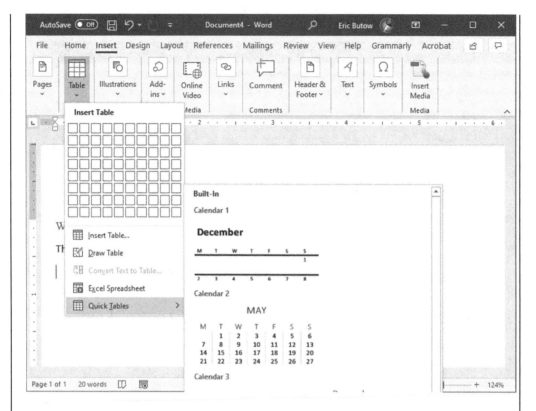

6. When you find a table that you like, click the style in the list. The table appears within your document so that you can start changing the text, add rows and columns, and make any other changes that you need to shine in front of that client (and your boss).

Converting Text to Tables

If you decide that some text in your document would be better presented as a table, Word has tools that make it easy to convert that text into a table when you follow these steps:

1. Select the text in the document.

2. Click the Insert menu option.

3. In the Insert ribbon, click the Table icon.

4. Click the Convert Cell To Table icon in the drop-down menu.

5. In the Convert Text To Table dialog box, shown in Figure 3.2, select the number of rows and columns that you want in the table in the Table Size section.

FIGURE 3.2   Convert Text To Table dialog box

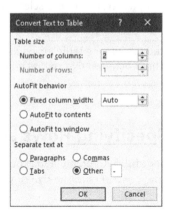

6. In the AutoFit Behavior section, you can set the specific width of a column or have Word do it by clicking one of the AutoFit options.

7. In the Separate Text At section, you can decide how to put each group of text in each table cell.

8. When you finish, click OK.

Now your text is in the table, though you may have to do some more tweaking to get it to appear the way you want it to.

Switching Tables to Text

As you work on a table, you may think that what's in a table may read better either in a paragraph of text or in a list. Or the amount of text may be so small that a table simply isn't needed. Whenever you want to change a table into text, start by clicking a cell in your table and then follow these steps:

1. Click the Layout menu option to the right of the Table Design option.

2. In the Layout ribbon, click the Select icon.

3. Click Select Table in the drop-down menu. Now all cells are gray, which means that Word has selected your entire table.

4. Click the Convert To Text icon in the Data section in the ribbon.

5. In the Convert Table To Text dialog box, choose if you want to separate text in each cell with paragraph marks, tabs (the default option), commas, or another character.

6. When you're done, click OK.

All your table text in the default paragraph style is selected in place of the table.

If there are nested tables (one table inside another table cell), the Convert Nested Tables check box is active so that you can convert those nested tables as well.

Creating Tables by Specifying Rows and Columns

The Insert Table grid gives you the ability to create a maximum table size of only 10 columns and 8 rows. If you need more control over the size of your columns when you create a table, follow these steps:

1. Place the cursor on the page where you want to insert the table.
2. Click the Insert menu option (if you haven't done so already).
3. Click the Table icon.
4. Click Insert Table in the drop-down menu, as shown in Figure 3.3.

FIGURE 3.3 Insert Table menu option

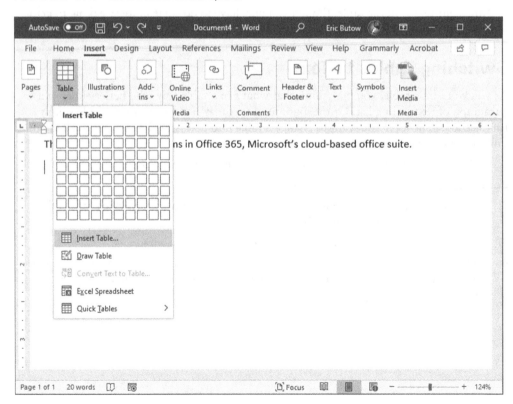

5. In the Insert Table dialog box (Figure 3.4), specify the number of columns and rows that you want in the Number Of Columns and Number Of Rows boxes, respectively. The default is five columns and two rows.

FIGURE 3.4 Insert Table dialog box

Now you can change the size of the columns in the AutoFit Behavior area. The default fixed column width is Auto, which means that Word takes care of it automatically. Here's what you can do to adjust the column and table widths:

- Click the up and down arrows to the right of the Fixed Column Width box to change the width of the box in tenths of an inch. The minimum width that you can set is 0.3 inches.
- Click AutoFit To Contents to have Word adjust the column width automatically.
- Click AutoFit To Window to have Word adjust the table width automatically.

You can save the settings for the next time you create a table by clicking the Remember Dimensions For New Tables check box. Once you're done, place your new table on the page by clicking OK.

EXERCISE 3.1

Creating a Table

1. Open a new document.

2. Type three words on five lines in the page.

3. Select all the text.

4. Convert the text to a table.

5. Press Enter.

6. Create a new table with three rows and two columns.

7. Type text into each table cell.

8. Click the Layout menu option to the right of the Table Design option.

9. In the Data section in the ribbon, click Convert To Text.

10. In the Convert Table To Text dialog box, keep Tabs as what you use to separate text and click OK.

11. Place the cursor below the selected text.

12. Insert a new table with 5 columns and 15 rows, and AutoFit the table to the window.

13. Click OK and enjoy your new table.

Modifying Tables

Word gives you a lot of power to modify your tables as you see fit. As in Microsoft Excel, you can sort text and/or numbers in a table. You can also take advantage of more tools to change the look of your table cells, rows, columns, and even the entire table.

You can also merge cells in your table. If you already have merged cells, or you have a cell that you think is too big, you can *split* it into two or more cells. And you can even split the entire table.

If your table is long, then it will likely appear on more than one page. To ensure that your readers know what they're looking at on each page, you can create a header row and tell Word to show that header row on every page in your table.

Sorting Table Data

A common *sorting* method for a table is to sort text in alphabetical order. Word also gives you the ability to sort by number and date. What is more, you can sort in multiple columns.

For example, you can sort the text in the first column alphabetically. After Word sorts all the text in the first column, it can sort the numbers in the second column.

After you create a table, click the table cell and then click the Layout menu option to the right of the Table Design option. In the Layout ribbon, click the Sort icon in the Data section, as shown in Figure 3.5.

In the Sort dialog box (see Figure 3.6), you can sort by three different columns. If the column has a header, then select the column name by clicking the Sort By box and then selecting the name in the drop-down list.

FIGURE 3.5 Sort icon

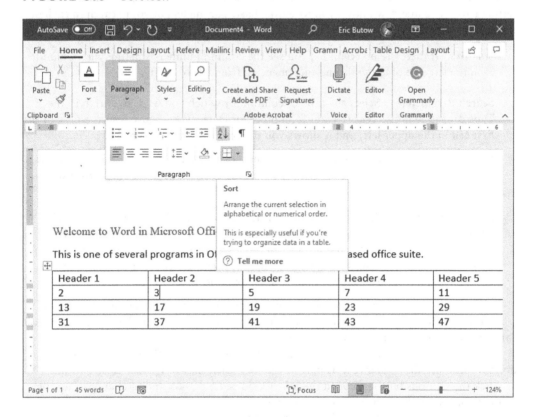

FIGURE 3.6 Sort dialog box

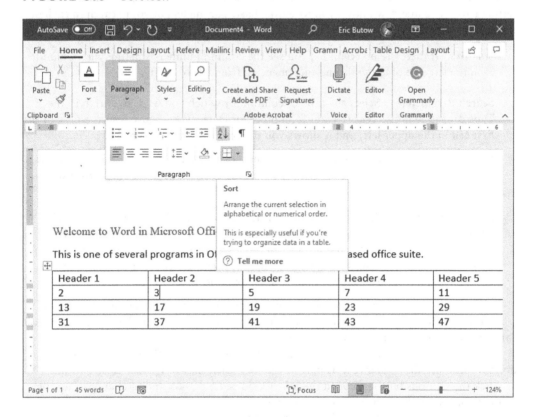

The Sort dialog box is almost a table itself, as it contains three setting columns and four setting rows. The first row allows you to set the basic parameters of your search in each of the three columns as follows:

Sort By   If there are no columns, you see the column numbers starting with Column 1 on the left side of the table and incrementing from left to right.

Search Parameters   Select the type of column for which you want to search in the Type drop-down list: Text (Default), Number, or Date. Word figures out the type of the first cell in the upper left, and it shows you the two types in the Type box.

In the Using box, sort by paragraphs, headings, or fields in a cell. When you click the box, the column type will determine what cell search types you see in the drop-down list.

Sort Order   Sorting in Ascending order is the default; that is, letters from A to Z. Click Descending in any of the three sort areas to sort from Z to A. If you sort by number, Word sorts by the first number in the text. For example, if you have the numbers 10 and 5 in a column, Word will list 10 first because 1 comes before 5. You can change this by sorting by number in the Type drop-down list.

The following two Then By rows allow you to sort by additional columns after Word sorts through the first column. For example, after you sort by name in the first column, you can sort by a number in the second column.

The Header Row button is selected by default at the bottom of the dialog box. If you don't want to use the header row as part of the sort, click the No Header Row button.

Click the Options button to open the Sort Options dialog box and to change other sort settings, such as making the sort text case sensitive.

When you're done, click OK. The table rows are reordered except for the header row, as shown in the example in Figure 3.7.

Configuring Cell Margins and Spacing

It's easy to configure margins and spacing around text in one or more table cells. All you have to do is click a cell and then change the column width either by using your mouse or by setting the height and width with the table's Layout ribbon.

FIGURE 3.7 The reordered table rows

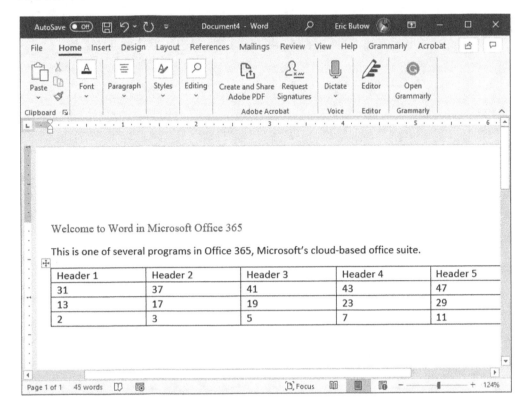

Use Your Mouse

To configure your cell width by clicking and dragging your mouse pointer, move the pointer on the right side of the column boundary you want to move until it becomes a resize pointer, which looks like a double-headed arrow, as shown in Figure 3.8.

Now drag the boundary until the column is the width you want and then release the mouse button.

If you want to get a precise measurement as you click and drag with your mouse, turn on the Word ruler (if it's not open already) by clicking the View menu option and then clicking the Ruler check box in the Show section in the ribbon.

FIGURE 3.8 Double-headed arrow icon

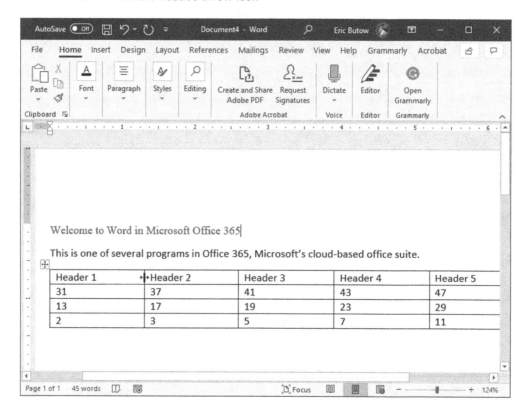

Once you see the ruler above your document (and just below the ribbon), click a cell in your table that you want to resize. The ruler shows trapezoid-shaped markers at the bottom edge of the ruler. These markers tell you where the cell begins and ends.

Move the cell border by clicking and dragging on the marker. When you hold down the Alt key as you click and drag, you see the exact width of the cell in inches, and the width changes as you move the marker to the left and right.

Set to a Specific Width

To change the width to a specific measurement, click a cell in the column that you want to resize. Click the Layout menu option to the right of the Table Design option.

The Cell Size section in the ribbon includes settings for the cell height and width in inches, and you can change the width by clicking in the Width box and typing the width in hundredths of an inch. Click the up or down arrow to the right of the box to increase or decrease, respectively, the width in increments by one-tenth of an inch.

Add or Change the Space Inside the Table

To add space inside your table, you can adjust cell margins or cell spacing. The difference? Cell margins are inside the table cell, and cell spacing is between cells. Here's how to add or change both cell margins and spacing:

1. Click a cell in the table.
2. Click the Layout menu option to the right of the Table Design option.
3. In the Layout ribbon, click the Cell Margins icon in the Alignment section.
4. The Table Options dialog box appears, as shown in Figure 3.9.

FIGURE 3.9   Table Options dialog box

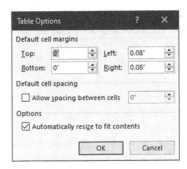

5. The Default Cell Margins area contains four boxes so that you can use to adjust the Top, Bottom, Left, and Right margins. Click the up or down arrow to the right of each box to increase or decrease, respectively, the margin by one-hundredth of an inch.
6. In the Default Cell Spacing area, click the Allow Spacing Between Cells check box, and then enter the measurement you want in the box. The default measurement is 0.01 inches.
7. Click OK.

The settings that you choose are available only in the active table. Any new table that you create will use that table's default settings.

Merging and Splitting Cells

There may be times when you need to *merge* multiple cells into one larger one. You may also find that when you have a cell with a lot of text, it's easier to read when you split that cell into two or more cells. Word makes it easy to do both tasks.

Merge Cells

You can combine two or more table cells located in the same row or column into a single cell. For example, you can merge several cells horizontally to create a heading row that spans several columns at the top of your table. Here's how:

1. Select the cells that you want to merge.

2. Click the Layout menu option to the right of the Table Design option.

3. In the Layout ribbon, click the Merge Cells icon in the Merge section, as shown in Figure 3.10.

FIGURE 3.10 Merge Cells menu option

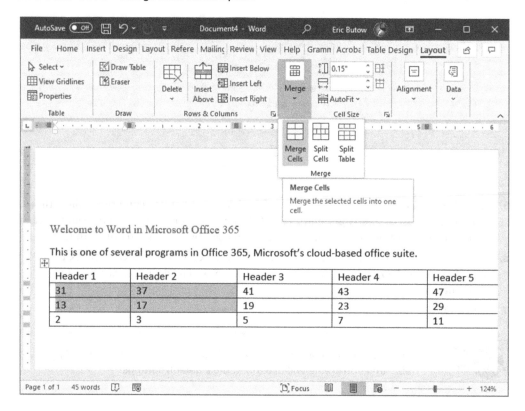

If there is text in several cells that you merged, you see several lines of text in the merged cell.

Split Cells

You can split one cell into multiple rows or columns by following these steps:

1. Click the cell, or select multiple cells, that you want to split in your table.

2. Click the Layout menu option to the right of the Table Design option.

3. In the Layout ribbon, click the Split Cells icon.

4. In the Split Cells dialog box, shown in Figure 3.11, type the number of columns and/or rows into which you want to split the cell.

FIGURE 3.11   Split Cells dialog box

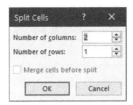

5. Click OK.

If you specify more rows and cells than there is text in the merged cell, then a lot of split cells won't have text in them.

Resizing Tables, Rows, and Columns

As you create a table, you may find that you want to resize one or more rows or columns. You may also need to resize the entire table.

Change Row Height

Configure the row height by moving your mouse pointer on the right side of the column boundary that you want to move until it becomes a resize pointer, which looks like a double-headed arrow with the arrows pointing up and down.

If you want to get a precise measurement as you click and drag with your mouse, click a cell in your table that you want to resize. The ruler on the left side of the Word window shows black boxes in the ruler that tell you where the cell begins and ends.

Move the cell border by clicking and dragging on the marker. When you hold down the Alt key as you click and drag, you see the exact width of the cell in inches, and the width changes as you move the marker up and down.

You can also set a specific height for all rows in a table. Here's how to do that:

1. Click a cell in the row that you want to change.

2. Click the Layout menu option to the right of the Table Design option.

3. In the Cell Size section, click the Height box. Word highlights the existing cell height, as shown in Figure 3.12.

FIGURE 3.12 Table Row Height box

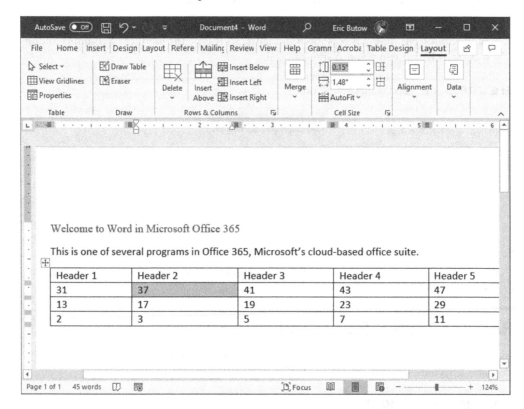

4. Type the cell height in the box. You can specify the height in hundredths of an inch if you want.

5. Press the Tab key.

The height for all rows in your table changes in your document. You can change the exact height by following the previous steps.

Click the up or down arrow to the right of the box to increase or decrease, respectively, the height in increments of one-tenth of an inch.

Resize a Column or Table Automatically with AutoFit

If you don't want to bother with resizing a column and/or table so that everything fits just right, let Word do it. Here's how:

1. Select a cell in the column you want to resize.
2. Click the Layout menu option to the right of the Table Design option.
3. In the Layout ribbon, click the AutoFit icon in the Cell Size section.
4. Click one of the following three sections, as shown in Figure 3.13:

FIGURE 3.13   AutoFit drop-down list

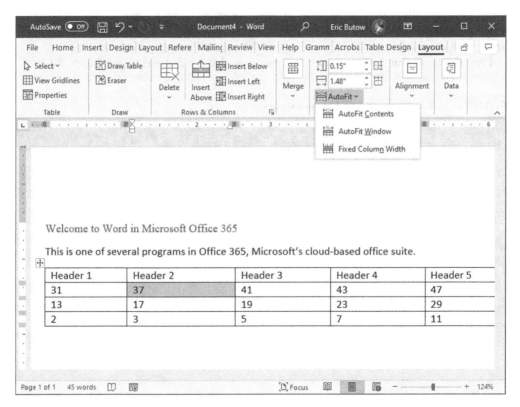

- Adjust the column width to the widest column by clicking AutoFit Contents.
- Adjust the table width to the full width of the page (minus the margins, of course) by clicking AutoFit Window.
- Keep Word from adjusting the column size as you type text by clicking Fixed Column Width.

Turn Off AutoFit

If you don't want AutoFit to set width in a column to fit the size of the text, here's how to turn it off:

1. Select a cell in the column that you want to resize.

2. Click the Layout menu option to the right of the Table Design option.

3. In the Layout ribbon, click the AutoFit icon in the Cell Size section.

4. Click Fixed Column Width in the drop-down menu.

Resize an Entire Table Manually

Word automatically creates a table so that it fits the entire width of the page. To resize, start by moving the cursor to the lower-right corner of the table. A white box appears at the lower right of the table.

Place the cursor on the box until it becomes a double-headed arrow (see Figure 3.14).

FIGURE 3.14   Double-headed arrow cursor

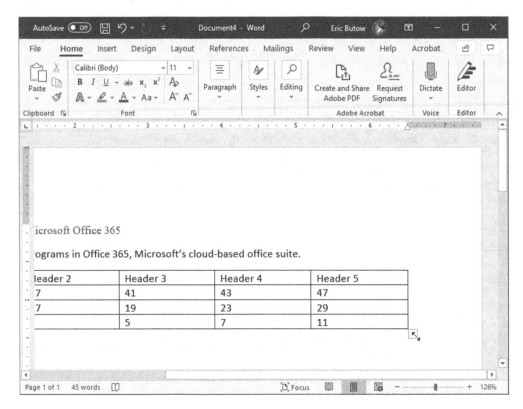

Now you can click and drag the box and watch the size of the table (and the contents in it) change. If you have text below the table, that text will move down as you stretch the table vertically.

Make Multiple Columns or Rows the Same Size

You may want to make more than one column or row the same size. For example, if you resize one column but you want that column and two columns to the left to be the same size, then you can make all three columns the same size in the space of the total width of those three columns.

Start by selecting the columns or rows that you want to make the same size. Figure 3.15 shows three selected columns. If you want to select noncontiguous rows or columns, hold down the Ctrl key as you select each row or column.

FIGURE 3.15   Selected columns

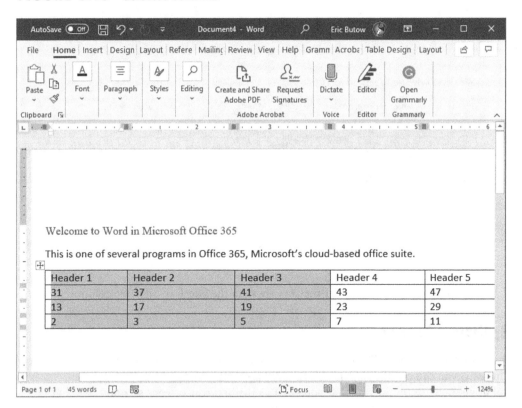

Next, click the Layout menu option to the right of the Table Design option. In the Layout ribbon in this example, click the Distribute Columns icon in the Cell Size section, as shown in Figure 3.16.

FIGURE 3.16   Distribute Columns icon

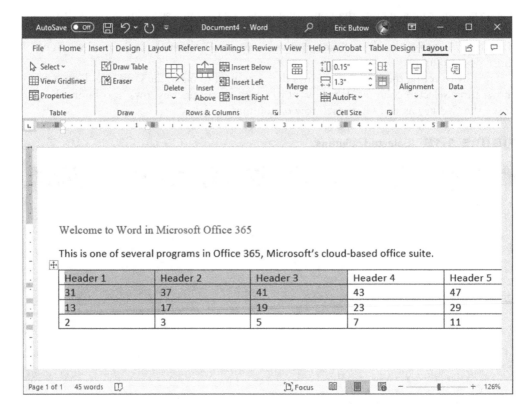

The columns change size so that they evenly span the width of all three columns.

Splitting Tables

Once you have a table in Word, you might decide to *split* that table into two or more tables. This way, you can create smaller tables or add text in between two tables.

Put your cursor on the row that you want as the first row of your second table. In the table shown in Figure 3.17, it's on the third row.

FIGURE 3.17   Cursor on third row

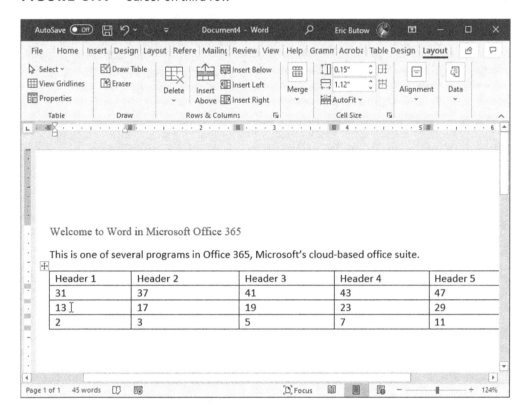

Now click the Layout menu option to the right of the Table Design option. In the Layout ribbon, click the Split Table icon in the Merge section (see Figure 3.18).

The row on which you placed the cursor is now the first row of the new table that appears below the other table. All rows underneath that first row appear underneath that first row.

FIGURE 3.18   Split Table icon

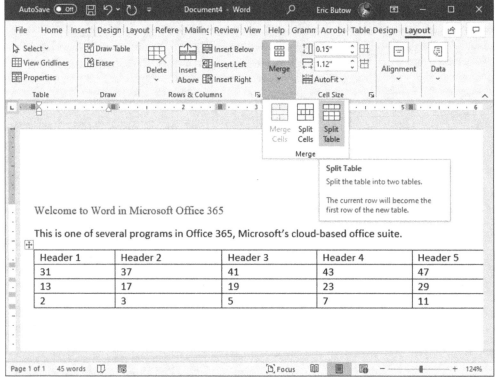

Configuring a Repeating Row Header

When you work with a table that is longer than the height of the page, cells that don't fit on that page appear on subsequent pages. You can set up the table so that the table header row or rows appear on each page automatically.

If your table has a header row, you can set up your table so that the header row appears at the top of each page, making your table easier to read. You can do this in one of two ways.

One way is to place the cursor somewhere in the header row of your table. Next, click the Layout menu option to the right of the Table Design option. In the Layout ribbon, click the Repeat Header Rows icon in the Data section (see Figure 3.19).

FIGURE 3.19   Repeat Header Rows icon

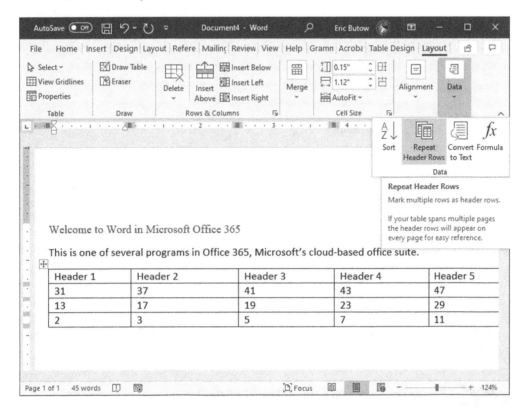

The other way is to right-click any cell in the header row of your table. In the context menu, click Table Properties. In the Table Properties dialog box, click the Row tab and then click the Repeat As Header Row At The Top Of Each Page check box, as shown in Figure 3.20.

FIGURE 3.20   Repeat At Header Row

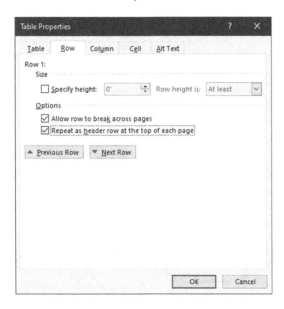

Click OK. No matter what method you choose, the header row will now appear on each page where your table is located.

As you work with headers, keep the following in mind:

- Repeated table headers are visible only in Print Layout view or when you print the document.

- If you change a table header on the first page, the header changes on all other pages as well. You can modify the table header only on the first page—the header rows on subsequent pages are locked.

- Although Word automatically repeats table headers on new pages that result from automatic page breaks, it does not repeat a header if you insert a manual page break in a table.

EXERCISE 3.2

Modifying a Table

1. Open a new document.

2. Add a new table with four columns and seven rows.

3. Populate the table with numbers.

4. Sort each column in ascending order.

5. Resize all the rows in the table.

6. Resize two of the columns in the table.

7. Split one of the merged cells.

8. Resize the columns with AutoFit.

9. Split the table into two tables.

Creating and Formatting Lists

Lists are an effective way of presenting information that readers can digest easily, as demonstrated in this book. Word includes many powerful tools to create lists easily and then format them so that they look the way you want them to appear.

Word provides two different types of lists. Each entry in a numbered list starts with a number, but you can also change the numbers to appear as letters. In a *bulleted list*, each entry starts with a special character, which is a black circle by default. You can change the special character to another special character, a symbol, or even a picture.

Structuring Paragraphs as Numbered and Bulleted Lists

An entry in a list, whether it's a few words or a few sentences, is treated as a paragraph. Word makes it easy to change a paragraph to a numbered list or a bulleted list.

Create a List

You don't need to do anything special to create a numbered or bulleted list.

Start a numbered list by typing 1, a period (.), a space, and then your text. When you finish typing your text, press Enter. Word formats the first entry in your list and places you on the next line in the numbered list with the number 2.

Create a bulleted list by typing an asterisk (*), a space, and then your text. When you're done typing, press Enter. The asterisk changes to a black circle and places you on the next line with another black circle to the left so that you can continue working on your list.

You can also start a numbered or bulleted list from within the Home ribbon. If you don't see it, click the Home menu option. In the ribbon, click the Bullets icon or the Numbered icon in the Paragraph section, as shown in Figure 3.21.

FIGURE 3.21   Bullets and Numbering icons

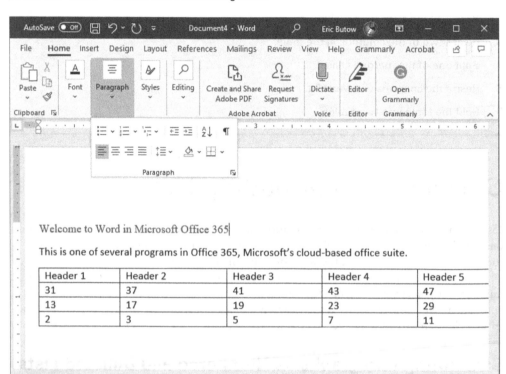

Now you see the number 1 or a bullet circle to the left of your cursor, and you can start typing your list. When you reach the last item in your list, press Enter twice to switch the bullets or numbering off.

Create a List from Existing Text

Using the Home ribbon, you can easily create a list from text you've already written. Start by selecting the text on the page, and then click the Bullets or Numbering icon in the Paragraph section. Each paragraph in the text appears as a separate number or bullet in the list.

You can continue the list by clicking the last item in the list and then pressing Enter. If the list is fine as is, click outside the selection.

Changing Bullet Characters and Number Formatting

You can change the format of the bullets or the numbers in a list by selecting from several different common *bullet characters* or *numbering* systems.

Bullets

Click one entry in your bulleted list. In the Home ribbon, click the down arrow to the right of the Bullets icon. The bullet style tiles appear in the drop-down list, as shown in Figure 3.22.

FIGURE 3.22   Bullet style tiles

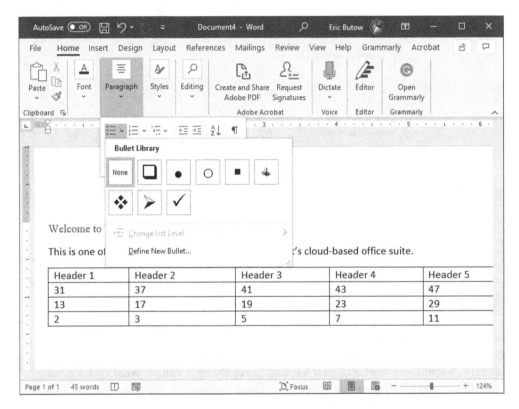

You can select a style in the Recently Used Bullets, Bullet Library, and Document Bullets sections. As you move the mouse pointer over each tile, all bullets in your list change so that you can see what the bullets look like in your list before you choose one. Once you find a bullet you like, click the tile. Or, if you don't want a bullet character in your list, click None.

Numbering

Click anywhere in your numbered list. In the Home ribbon, click the down arrow to the right of the Numbering icon. The number style tiles appear in the drop-down list (see Figure 3.23).

FIGURE 3.23   Number style tiles

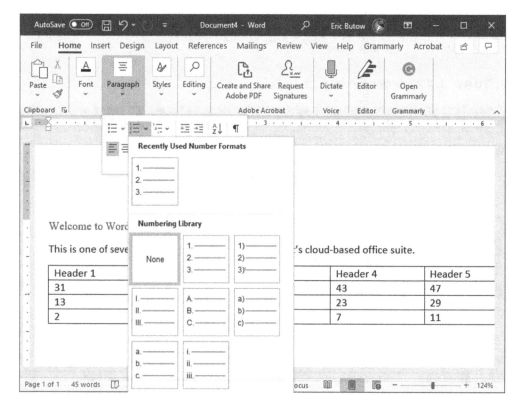

You can select a numbering style in the Recently Used Number Formats, Numbering Library, and Document Number Formats sections. As you move the mouse pointer over each tile, the number format in your list changes so that you can see what each format looks like in your list before you choose one. Once you find a format you like, click the tile. If you don't want numbers in your list, click None.

Defining Custom Bullet Characters and Number Formatting

The common bullet characters or number formatting may not be to your liking. No worries; Word has a number (ahem) of other formats from which you may choose.

Bullets

You may need custom bullet characters or symbols to represent what you do better. For example, if your company uses a triangle in its logo, you can change your bullet characters to triangle symbols.

Here's how to create a new bulleted list with a symbol:

1. Place the cursor where you want to add the bulleted list in your document.

2. Click the Home menu option if you're not there already.

3. In the Home ribbon, click the down arrow to the right of the Bullets icon in the Paragraph section.

4. Click Define New Bullet in the drop-down menu.

5. In the Define New Bullet dialog box, as shown in Figure 3.24, click Symbol.

FIGURE 3.24   Define New Bullet dialog box

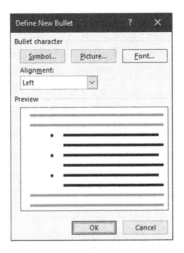

6. In the Symbol dialog box, scan the list of symbols and then click the symbol you want to use.

7. Click OK.

8. In the Define New Bullet dialog box, click OK.

The first bulleted list entry with your new symbol appears on the screen. The symbol also appears in the Recently Used Bullets and Bullets Library sections in the Bullets drop-down menu.

Numbering

Here's how to access all the numbering formats in the Define New Number format dialog box:

1. Place the cursor where you want to add the numbered list in your document.

2. Click the Home menu option if you're not there already.

3. In the Home ribbon, click the down arrow to the right of the Numbering icon in the Paragraph section.

4. Click Define New Number Format in the drop-down menu.

5. In the Define New Number Format dialog box, as shown in Figure 3.25, change the style by clicking the down arrow next to the Number Style box.

FIGURE 3.25 Define New Number Format dialog box

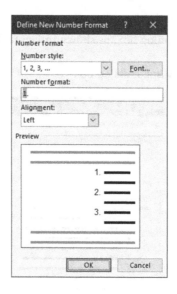

6. Select from one of the numbered styles, text styles, or other chronological format such as 1st, 2nd, and 3rd.

7. Click the Font button to change the numbering font, color, and other styles.

8. Click OK to close the Font dialog box.

9. If desired, add other text after the number, such as parenthetical text, in the Number Format text box.

10. Change the number alignment by clicking the Alignment box and then selecting Left, Centered, or Right in the drop-down list. You can see the results of the alignment change in the Preview box.

11. Click OK.

The numbered list in your document now displays its new numbering format. The new format also appears as an icon in the Recently Used Number Formats and Numbering Library sections in the Numbering drop-down menu.

Increasing and Decreasing List Levels

You can change list levels for both bulleted and numbered lists by indenting an entry in your list. As you change list levels, the bullet or number format changes to match the built-in level styles for each format.

View the format of each list level and apply a new list level by clicking the list entry to which you want to apply the new level.

Next, click the Home menu option if you haven't already. Depending on the type of list, click the down arrow to the right of the Bullets or Numbering icon in the Home ribbon.

In the drop-down menu, move the mouse pointer over Change List Level. The submenu appears, as shown in Figure 3.26.

FIGURE 3.26   Change List Level menu

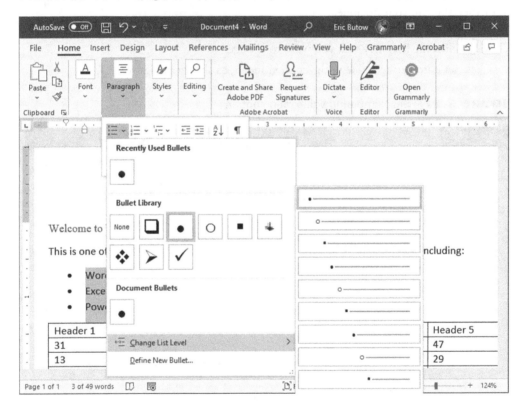

The list shows nine levels, starting with the first level at the top. Each level shows you the bullet character and indent spacing used for that level. Apply a level to your item by clicking the level in the list. If you're changing a list entry with a lower level, click a higher level in the list. Your entry appears with the applied list level. All other entries in the list are unaffected.

When you want to change the list level for multiple entries, or for the entire list, select the entries in the list and then follow the steps in this section.

If you have a custom bullet style, you will see the same bullet no matter the list level.

Restarting and Continuing List Numbering

As you work with numbered lists, you may find that Word can get confused about starting a new list or continuing a previous one. It may be tempting to change numbers in a list manually, but that will only cause more confusion (and headaches) when you work with a list further along in your document.

So, here's how to change numbering values in Word the right way:

1. Right-click the list entry that you want to change.
2. Click Set Numbering Value in the context menu, as shown in Figure 3.27.

FIGURE 3.27   Set Numbering Value menu option

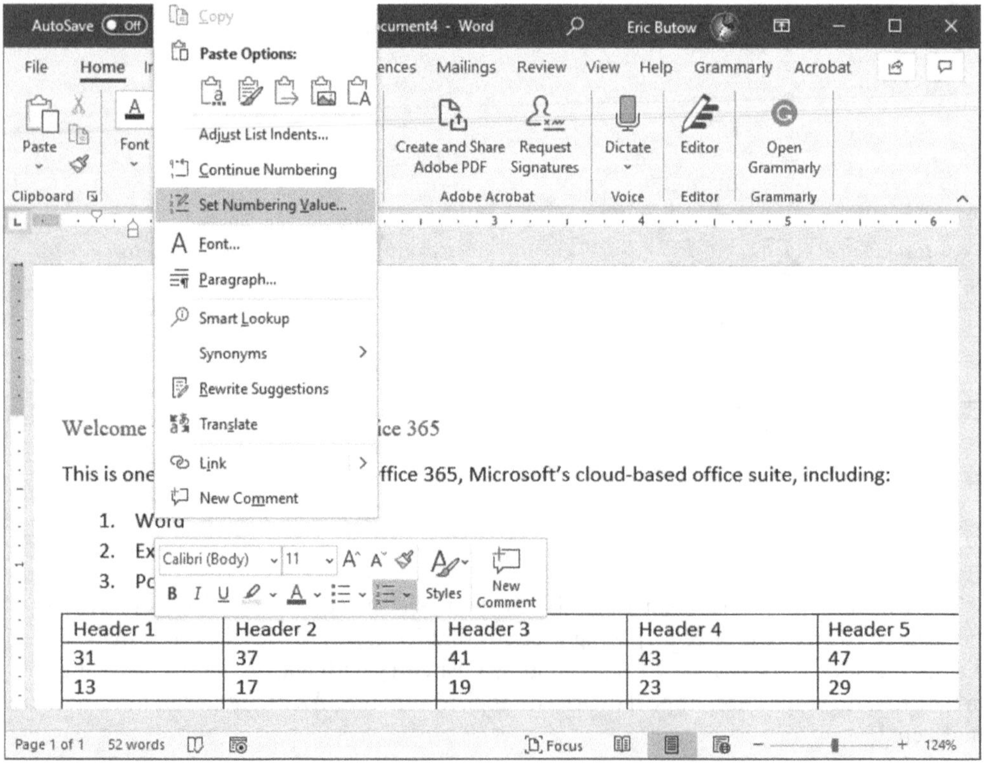

3. In the Set Numbering Value dialog box (see Figure 3.28), type the new value in the Set Value To text box.

FIGURE 3.28 Set Numbering Value dialog box

The list entry shows the new number you gave it. Entries that follow your newly renumbered one will continue from that new number in sequential order.

Changing number values is especially useful when you have two lists (or more) separated by other text with different formats. If you want one list to continue the numbering of the previous list, all you have to do is right-click the first entry in the numbered list that you want to renumber, and then click Continue Numbering in the context menu, as shown in Figure 3.29.

FIGURE 3.29 Continue Numbering option

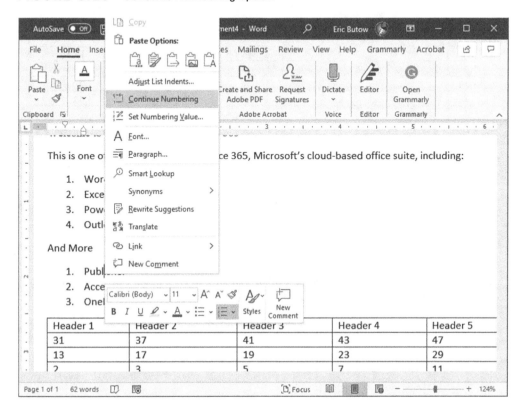

Your list has the number that follows the last number in the previous number list. Word also renumbers subsequent entries in the list so that they continue in sequential order.

Setting Starting Number Values

If you need to restart one entry in your numbered list with the numbered one, or if you broke up one list into two and the second list continues the numbering from the previous list, you can reset the starting value number in a list entry.

Start by right-clicking the list entry that you want to change to 1. In the context menu that appears (see Figure 3.30), click the Restart At 1 menu option.

FIGURE 3.30 Restart At 1 menu option

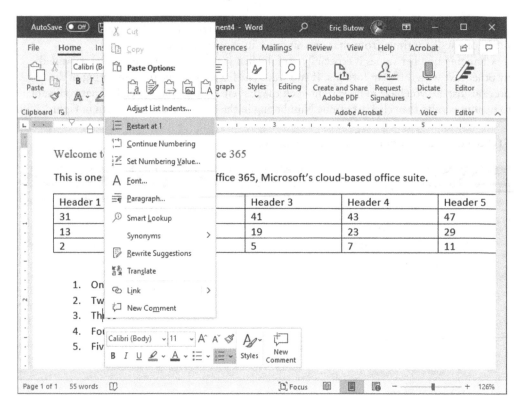

The entry appears with the number 1, and all list entries under that new entry number 1 continue with the numbers 2, 3, and so on.

EXERCISE 3.3

Formatting Your List

1. Open a blank document.

2. Create one bulleted list with four items.

3. Press Enter three times, and then create one numbered list with four items.

4. Click anywhere in the bulleted list and change the bullet style to a check mark.

5. Click anywhere in the bulleted list and change the number format to A, B, C.

6. Click the second item in the bulleted list and then change the list level to Level 2.

7. Click the last item in the numbered list and then change the list level to Level 3.

8. Create a new numbered list after the numbered list with at least one blank line between the two numbered lists.

9. Click the first entry in the second numbered list and continue the line numbering from the previous list.

Summary

This chapter started by showing you how to create a table from selected text. Then you saw how to reverse the process and convert a table into text. You also learned how to use Word table tools to create a table from scratch.

After you created a table, you learned how to modify tables. I discussed how to sort data in a table. Next, you learned how to modify the look and feel of your tables, including changing the cell margins; spacing, merging, and splitting cells; and resizing parts of your table. I discussed when you would need to split a table in two and how to do that. And you learned how to create a repeating row header in case your table is longer than one page and you want the header to appear at the top of each page.

Next I discussed how to create and format text lists, and I started with converting paragraphs into numbered and bulleted lists. You learned how to change and define bullet characters and format numbered lists. After that, I discussed how to increase and decrease list levels in a list.

Finally, you learned several important things about managing numbered lists, including how to restart and continue list numbering properly as well as how to set starting number values.

Key Terms

bullet characters

bulleted list

cells

columns

header row

list levels

merge

number formatting

numbering

Rows

Sorting

Split

Tables

Exam Essentials

Understand how to convert text to tables, and vice versa. Know how to use the Table option in the Insert menu to convert text to tables, or to switch tables back to text.

You must understand structuring paragraphs as numbered and bulleted lists; changing bullet characters and number formatting; defining custom bullet characters and number formatting; increasing and decreasing list levels; restarting and continuing list numbering; and setting starting number values.

Know how to specify rows and columns. Understand how to add a specific number of rows and columns in a table.

Understand how to modify a table. Know how to sort data in a table; change margins and spacing in a cell; merge and split cells and tables; and resize elements of a table, including rows, columns, and the entire table. You also need to know how to configure a repeating row header.

Know how to create numbered and bulleted lists. Understand the difference between bulleted lists and numbered lists, and how to create each one.

Understand how to format numbered and bulleted lists. Know how to use formatting tools to change the look and feel of bulleted lists and numbered lists.

Be able to change list levels. Know how to increase and decrease the levels in a bulleted list and a numbered list.

Know how to manage list numbering. Know how to change the numbering in a list to ensure each number in the list continues sequentially. You need to understand how to set values in a new numbered list so that it does not continue numbering from the previous list.

Review Questions

1. How do you create a table with built-in styles?
   - **A.** Click the Table icon in the Insert ribbon.
   - **B.** Open the Styles panel.
   - **C.** Click the Insert ribbon, click Table, and then move the mouse pointer over Quick Tables in the drop-down menu.
   - **D.** Click the Columns icon in the Layout menu.

2. How do you create a table with three columns and seven rows?
   - **A.** Click the Table option in the Insert ribbon to open a dialog box.
   - **B.** Click the Table option in the Insert ribbon and move the mouse pointer over the grid.
   - **C.** Click the Table option and then click Draw Table.
   - **D.** Click the Table option in the Insert ribbon and then click Insert Table.

3. In what order is a sort from the letters Z to A?
   - **A.** Ascending
   - **B.** Alphabetical
   - **C.** Descending
   - **D.** Backward

4. How do you see the exact measurement of a table row or column when you resize it using the mouse?
   - **A.** Holding down the Alt key as you drag
   - **B.** Holding down the Ctrl key as you drag
   - **C.** Looking at the ruler above the document
   - **D.** Holding down Ctrl+Shift as you drag

5. How do you resize a table or columns to fit the size of your content?
   - **A.** Quick Tables
   - **B.** Orientation
   - **C.** Size
   - **D.** AutoFit

6. What menu options appear when you click inside a table?
   - **A.** Table Design and Layout
   - **B.** Shape Layout

    C.   Format and Table Design

    D.   Chart Design

7. What types of bullets can you add to a list?

    A.   Symbols and fonts

    B.   Symbols, fonts, and pictures

    C.   Special characters

    D.   Asterisks

8. What search parameter types can you use for sorting table contents?

    A.   Text and numbers

    B.   Special characters

    C.   Text, numbers, and dates

    D.   Text and symbols

9. How do you create a bulleted list as you type text?

    A.   Press the period (.) key.

    B.   Press the plus (+) key.

    C.   Press the asterisk (*) key.

    D.   Press the caret (^) key.

10. Why shouldn't you change the numbers in a list manually?

    A.   Because Word will stop running

    B.   Because Word will convert the numbered list to text

    C.   Because your document will close without saving

    D.   Because Word will lose track of what you've done and get confused

Chapter

4

Building References

MICROSOFT EXAM OBJECTIVES COVERED IN THIS CHAPTER:

✓ **Create and manage references**

  ✓ **Create and manage reference elements**

- Insert footnotes and endnotes

- Modify footnote and endnote properties

- Create and modify bibliography citation sources

- Insert citations for bibliographies

  ✓ **Create and manage reference tables**

- Insert tables of contents

- Customize tables of contents

- Insert bibliographies

When you first learned about writing *references* in school, you may have realized that it would help you later in your studies when you wrote a lot of papers. Now that you're into your professional career, you may be surprised by how much you need to find references for your documents and credit their source properly so that you don't get into trouble with your legal department (and your boss).

Word includes all of the tools that you need to add and manage reference elements. In this chapter, I will talk about adding those elements, including footnotes, endnotes, citations, and bibliographies. You also don't have to worry about formatting your references correctly, because Word comes with styles for 12 different writing style manuals.

I also discuss adding a *table of contents (TOC)* to a document so that readers can jump to different locations in your document easily.

Creating and Managing Referencing Elements

Three types of reference elements that you can add into a Word document are as follows:

Footnotes: Notes of references, explanations, or comments placed at the bottom of a page.

Endnotes: Like footnotes, with the key difference being that all of the endnotes are placed at the end of the document.

Citations: References to entries in a bibliography. Later in this chapter, you'll learn more about what a bibliography is and how to add one.

These references not only help give your readers complete information, but also place supplemental information out of the way so that readers can refer to it at their leisure.

Inserting Footnotes and Endnotes

Word makes it easy to add one or more footnotes at the bottom of the page where you insert the footnotes.

Add Footnote

Here's how to add a footnote on a page:

1. Place the cursor where you want to add the footnote.
2. Click the References menu option.
3. In the ribbon, click Insert Footnote in the Footnotes section (see Figure 4.1).

FIGURE 4.1   Insert Footnote option

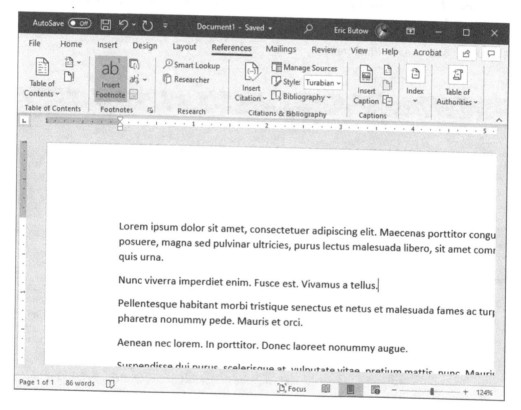

The footnote number appears at the insertion point in superscript format. The footnote itself appears in the page footer with a line above it to set it off from the rest of the text. The cursor is blinking within the footnote so that you can enter the footnote text.

When you're done, click the cursor anywhere else in the document to continue editing your document. If you need to edit the footnote again, all you need to do is place the cursor within the footnote text.

As you add and edit text, the footnote stays on the page until the text that includes the footnotes moves to a different page. The footnote moves with it.

Place Endnote

Adding endnotes is as easy as adding footnotes. Just follow these steps:

1. Place the cursor where you want to add the endnote.

2. Click the References menu option.

3. In the ribbon, click the Insert Endnote icon in the Footnotes section, as shown in Figure 4.2.

FIGURE 4.2   Insert Endnote icon

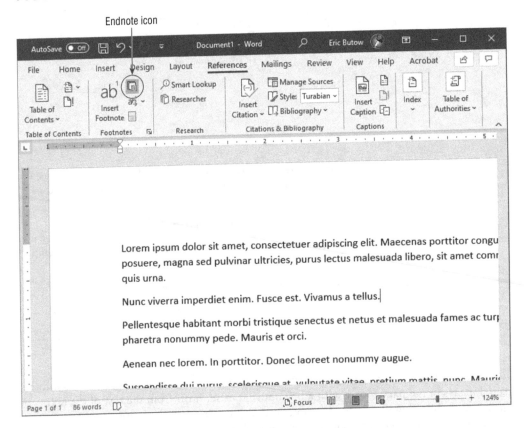

Word places your cursor within the endnote at the end of the document so that you can type it.

Endnotes are within the text, not in the footer. Word inserts a line above it to set it off from the rest of the text. The cursor is blinking within the end so that you can type it.

When you finish typing it, you must go back to the page where you inserted the endnote. The endnote number is in superscript style, just as in a footnote.

Now you can click the cursor anywhere else in the document to finish editing.

How do you delete a footnote or endnote? Select the superscript number in the text that's connected to the footnote or endnote, and then press Delete on your keyboard. The footnote or endnote disappears.

Modifying Footnote and Endnote Properties

There is no style for footnotes and endnotes. Word simply uses its default 10-point Calibri font.

If you want to change the font, double-click anywhere in the footnote text. In the menu that appears above the text, as shown in Figure 4.3, select the font, size, and more. When you change the size, the superscript number size changes, too.

FIGURE 4.3   Pop-up menu for changing the footnote style

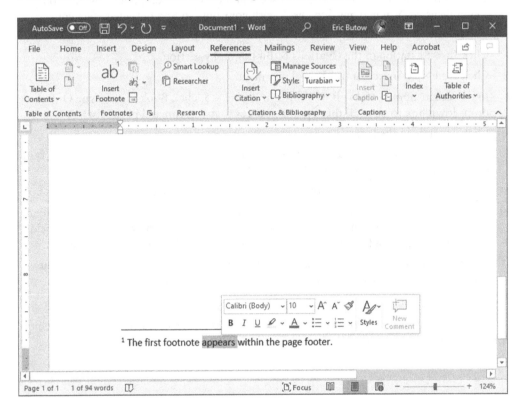

Creating and Modifying Bibliography Citation Sources

A *bibliography* is what the Merriam-Webster online dictionary defines as "the history, identification, or description of writings or publications." Those writings and publications can be books, websites, films, and other types of media.

You can cite these works by adding them as sources to your document, and Word supports 16 different specific source types. Once you create a source, Word makes it easy for you to insert a citation in one or several locations in your document.

Create a Source

Before you cite a source, you must add it to your Word document. Here's how:

1. Place the cursor where you want to add the citation in the document.
2. Click the References menu option.
3. In the Citations & Bibliography section in the ribbon, click the down arrow to the right of Turabian to change the style guide.
4. Select the style to use for your citation in the drop-down list, as shown in Figure 4.4.

    Turabian is the default because it's widely used for academic papers, but Chicago (for Chicago Manual of Style) is the guide used commonly for book publishing and so it's comprehensive. You may need to check with your boss to find out what style your company uses, if any.

5. Click Insert Citation in the Citations & Bibliography section.
6. Click Add New Source in the drop-down menu.
7. In the Create Source dialog box, shown in Figure 4.5, click Book in the Type Of Source drop-down box to view all the types of sources that you can add in the list.
8. Click a source in the list.

    The information that you can add in the fields depends on the style type and what type of source you add. For this example, I used the default, Book.

9. Type the author name by using the suggested format near the bottom of the dialog box.
10. After you add all the information, you can view the fields to add to the bibliography by clicking the Show All Bibliography Fields check box. A book reference has many fields, including the state and country, edition number, and number of pages in the book.
11. Word fills in the tag name with the first few characters of the author name, but you can change this by clicking the Tag Name box and typing the new name.
12. When you finish, click OK.

The citation appears in parentheses at the insertion point. You'll learn how to add a citation that references your source later in this chapter.

FIGURE 4.4   Writing styles list

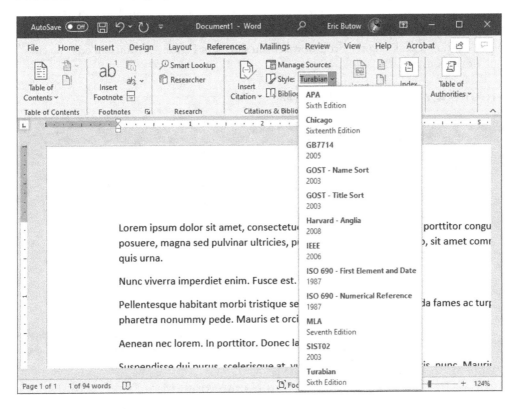

FIGURE 4.5   Create Source dialog box

Modify a Source

If you ever need to change source information, such as to change spelling or add more information, click anywhere within the citation and then click the down arrow to the right of the citation text. Using the drop-down menu shown in Figure 4.6, you can edit the citation or the source.

FIGURE 4.6   Citation drop-down menu

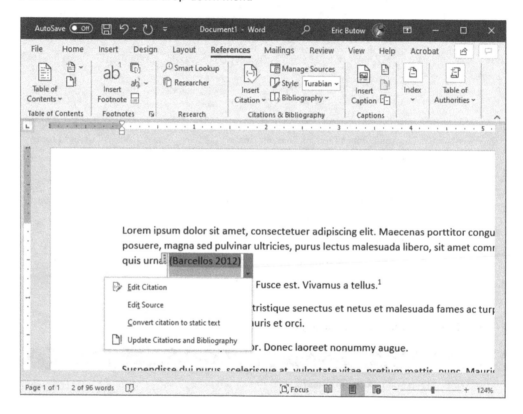

Edit Citation

Click Edit Citation for a quick edit. In the Edit Citation dialog box, add the page that you're referencing by typing it in the Pages box.

If you want to hide the author, year, and/or title of the work you're referencing, click the appropriate check box.

When you're done, click OK. The document reflects the changes that you made.

Edit Source

Click Edit Source in the menu. The Edit Source dialog box appears so that you can edit and add citation information as you learned to do when you created a citation. When you're done, click OK. The document reflects the changes you made.

Inserting Citations for Bibliographies

When you click Insert Citation in the ribbon, the citation appears in the drop-down list (see Figure 4.7) so that you can easily add it to other locations in your document.

FIGURE 4.7   Added citation in drop-down list

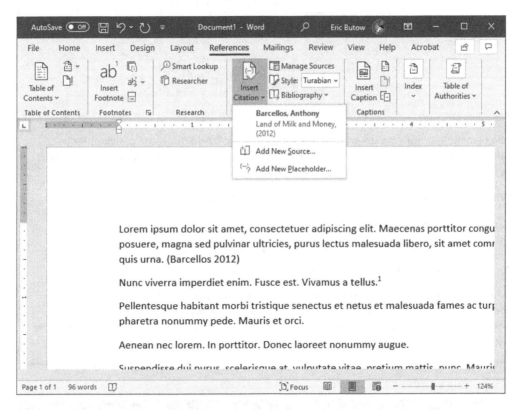

Add a Citation Placeholder

If you don't have all the information you need yet because you're waiting on a coworker to send some to you, Word makes it easy to put in a placeholder so that you don't forget where each of your coworker's citations will go. Here's what to do:

1. Place your cursor where you want to add the placeholder on the page.

2. Click the References menu option.

3. In the References ribbon, click the Insert Citation icon.

4. In the drop-down menu, click Add New Placeholder.

5. In the Placeholder Name dialog box, press Backspace on your keyboard to delete the default name in the name box and then type the new one.

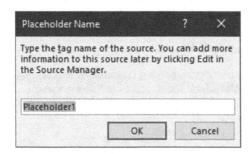

6. Click OK.

The placeholder appears where you placed your cursor. Add the same placeholder in other location(s) in your text by adding it as you would a citation; the placeholder name is in the Insert Citation drop-down list.

When you have the source information, here's what to do next:

1. Click the placeholder name.

2. Click the down arrow to the right of the placeholder name.

3. In the drop-down menu, click Edit Source.

You can add the new source information as you would any other source. After you add the new source, the information appears within the placeholder instead of the place-holder name. Word also updates any other citations that have the same placeholder name with the new citation.

EXERCISE 4.1

Insert a Footnote, Source, and Citation

1. Click the location in your document where you want to add a footnote.

2. Add a new footnote.

3. Click another location on the same page in your document where you want to add the second footnote.

4. Add the second footnote.

5. Change the font in both footnotes to Times New Roman.

6. Create a source for one of your favorite books that includes the author, title, and publication year.

7. Place your cursor on another page in your document where you want to add a citation to a source.

8. Insert the citation.

9. Add the publication year to the citation.

Working with Referencing Tables

You can add two different types of reference sources in your document, which Microsoft calls reference tables:

> A *table of contents (TOC)*: This gives your readers an easy way to find information in your document. Word scans your TOC for text with a Heading style, and then adds it into the correct location within your TOC.

> A *bibliography*: This usually appears as an appendix at the end of a document so that people who want to see the works you referenced can get all the information concisely.

Word makes it easy to add a TOC and a bibliography from the References menu ribbon.

Inserting Tables of Contents

A TOC usually appears on the first page(s) of a document. So, place the cursor at the beginning of your document, and then follow these steps to add a TOC:

1. Click the References menu option.

2. In the Table of Contents section in the ribbon, click Table Of Contents.

3. In the drop-down menu, shown in Figure 4.8, click one of the two built-in automatic table styles that automatically creates a TOC based on styles in your document. Alternatively, you can click Manual Table to add a TOC that you can edit independently of the content. For this example, I used Automatic Table 1.

Level 1 is flush left, Level 2 is indented once, Level 3 is indented twice, and so on, up to Level 9. The automatic table styles add levels based on the Heading style number—that is, Heading 1 through Heading 9.

Contents appear with the Automatic Table 1 style format at the insertion point in the document.

FIGURE 4.8 TOC styles menu

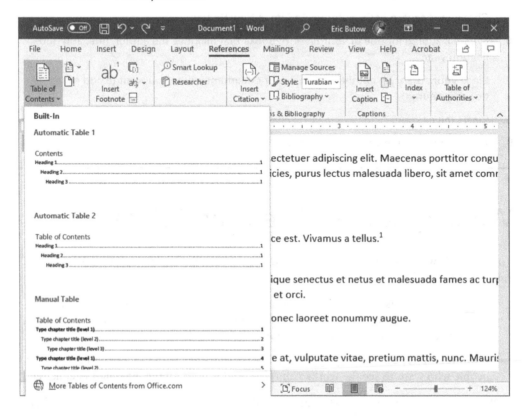

 In the Table Of Contents drop-down list, click More Tables Of Contents From Office.com to check whether Microsoft has added any new styles lately.

Customizing Tables of Contents

When you add a TOC, it reflects the contents of the document. Word doesn't update the TOC automatically after you make changes elsewhere in your document. You can customize your TOC in one of two ways.

Start by clicking anywhere in the TOC. A box appears around your TOC and two buttons appear at the top of the box. A button with a page icon is on the left and a button that says Update Table is on the right.

Change Style or Remove TOC

When you click the down arrow to the right of the page icon, the Built-In drop-down menu appears (see Figure 4.9).

In the Built-In drop-down menu, select a new built-in style or remove the TOC.

FIGURE 4.9 TOC styles in the Built-In menu

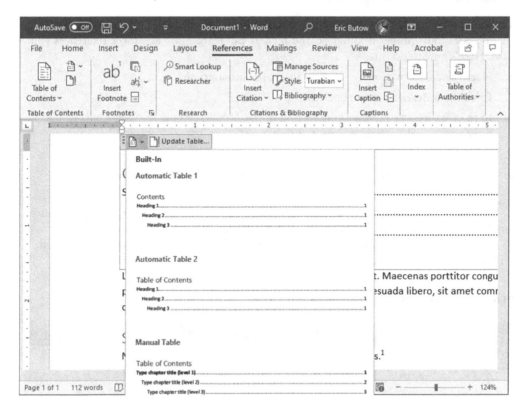

In the drop-down menu, you can select a new built-in style, and after you click the style tile, your TOC reflects the new style.

When you select Remove Table Of Contents from the menu, the TOC disappears.

Update Table

After you click Update Table, the Update Table Of Contents dialog box allows you to choose to update only the page numbers by default. Do this if headings are still at the same level but on different pages. When you click OK in the dialog box, Word updates the page numbers in the TOC.

Click the Update Entire Table button if you have new heading text, if some heading text has new levels, and/or you deleted some heading text. After you click OK, Word updates the entire TOC, including page numbers.

Change the Styles in the TOC

Word adds TOC styles for each level automatically when you add the TOC. You can access these styles by pressing Alt+Ctrl+Shift+S to open the Styles list. The styles are listed TOC 1 through TOC 9, where the number is the TOC level. Even if you delete the TOC, the styles remain in case you add another TOC in your document.

Adding Bibliographies

You know how to add a citation, but now you need to add the bibliography so that the citation goes to its proper destination and readers can learn more about the references you used. Here's how to do this:

1. Place the cursor where you want to insert the bibliography.

2. Click the References menu option.

3. In the Citations & Bibliography section in the ribbon, change the style guide in the same way you did when you created a citation.

4. Click Bibliography.

5. Select the built-in bibliography style that you want from the drop-down menu, as shown in Figure 4.10.

Click Insert Bibliography at the bottom of the menu to add your bibliography without any heading text that is included in the built-in styles.

No matter what kind of bibliography you insert, Word allows you to edit the inserted bibliography as you see fit.

FIGURE 4.10   Bibliography styles

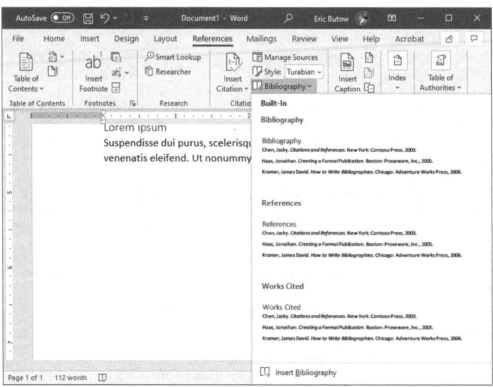

EXERCISE 4.2

Adding a TOC and Bibliography

1. Place your cursor at the beginning of your document.

2. Add a TOC with your preferred style.

3. Change the TOC 1 style to Times New Roman bold.

4. Add some more text to your document that includes at least one line with a heading style.

5. Update the TOC.

6. Go to the last page of your document and place the cursor at the end of the page.

7. Add a bibliography with the Chicago writing style and the Bibliography format.

Summary

This chapter started with a discussion about adding and modifying footnotes and endnotes. I followed up by discussing how to add and change citation sources and then insert them for your bibliography of references.

Next, I discussed how to add two types of reference tables. The table of contents (TOC) usually appears at the beginning of the document and contains a list of text with heading styles so that readers can go to a section in your document quickly.

I concluded by talking about adding a bibliography of your sources with the correct style prescribed by a writing style guide that you can select from the References menu ribbon.

Key Terms

bibliography

citations

endnotes

footnotes

references

table of contents (TOC)

Exam Essentials

Understand how to add footnotes and endnotes.   Footnotes, which appear at the bottom of the page, are great ways to give readers more information about text in your document without that additional information getting in the way. If you have too many footnotes in a page or in a document, consider putting those notes at the end of your chapter by using endnotes. Word gives you the tools you need to add and modify both footnotes and endnotes.

Know how to create and modify bibliography sources.   Before you create a bibliography, you need to understand how to use Word tools to create sources you'll cite throughout your document. Then you need to know how to modify the source format to give readers the information you think they should see in each citation.

Understand how to add a citation for a bibliography.   Know how to select from an existing citation easily so that you can add the same citation in several different locations in your document.

Be able to add and modify a table of contents.   Understand how to add and customize a table of contents (TOC) to make it easy for readers to find the sections of text that they want to read.

Understand how to create a bibliography.   Know how to create a bibliography at the end of your document with the correct writing style format so that you properly document references that you used to support the text in your document.

Review Questions

1. What menu option do you click to add a footnote or endnote?
   A. Insert
   B. Design
   C. References
   D. Home

2. How do you change the style of a footnote or endnote?
   A. Select a style in the Home ribbon.
   B. Select the footnote text, and then change the properties in the pop-up menu.
   C. Click the Design layout option to change the properties in the ribbon.
   D. Click the layout option to change the indents, spacing, and other styles.

3. Why do you set a writing style before creating a citation?
   A. Because you need to know what a writing style is
   B. Because you can't add a citation otherwise
   C. Because the style affects the format of the citation
   D. You don't have to because the default Turabian style is good enough.

4. How do you add a page number to an existing citation?
   A. Click the citation, click the down arrow to the right of the citation, and then click Edit Citation.
   B. Type the number after the author name within the parentheses.
   C. Click Manage Sources in the References ribbon.
   D. Click the Insert menu option, and then click Page Number in the Insert ribbon.

5. How do you add a placeholder for a citation that you plan to add later?
   A. Click the Insert menu option, and then click Bookmark in the ribbon.
   B. Click the References menu option, and then click Manage Sources in the ribbon.
   C. In the References ribbon, click Mark Citation.
   D. In the References ribbon, click Insert Citation and then click Add New Placeholder.

6. What is a TOC level?
   A. A means of determining how text with certain heading styles should appear in your TOC
   B. How many times each entry in the TOC is indented
   C. How Word keeps track of all the different TOC elements
   D. How Word determines the TOC layouts from which you can choose

7. How do you change a style in a TOC?

   A. Click the References menu option, and then click Update Table in the ribbon.

   B. Change the TOC in the Styles pane.

   C. Click the TOC in the document.

   D. Click the Design menu option, and then change the theme in the ribbon.

8. Why do you need to update a TOC?

   A. You don't, because Word updates it automatically as you type.

   B. Because it's a good idea to keep your TOC up to date

   C. Because Word doesn't update the TOC automatically with new page numbers and headers

   D. You don't, because Word automatically updates the TOC when you save the document.

9. Why do you need to change the writing style before you add a bibliography?

   A. You don't, because the default Turabian style is the only one used for bibliographies.

   B. Because no writing style is applied before you write a bibliography

   C. Because Word formats any bibliography you add with the correct writing style formats

   D. You don't, because the default bibliography options already contain the correct writing style.

10. What are the three types of bibliography templates from which you can choose?

   A. Turabian, Chicago, APA

   B. APA, MLA, Chicago

   C. Last Name, Date, Title of Work

   D. Bibliography, References, Works Cited

Chapter

5

Adding and Formatting Graphic Elements

MICROSOFT EXAM OBJECTIVES COVERED IN THIS CHAPTER:

✓ **Insert and format graphic elements**

- Insert illustrations and text boxes
    - Insert shapes
    - Insert pictures
    - Insert 3D models
    - Insert SmartArt graphics
    - Insert screenshots and screen clippings
    - Insert text boxes
- Format illustrations and text boxes
    - Apply artistic effects
    - Add picture effects and picture styles
    - Remove picture backgrounds
    - Format graphic elements
    - Format SmartArt graphics
    - Format 3D models
- Add text to graphic elements
    - Add and modify text in text boxes
    - Add and modify text in shapes
    - Add and modify SmartArt graphic content
- Modify graphic elements
    - Position objects
    - Wrap text around objects
    - Add alternative text to objects for accessibility

Word has taken plenty of features from desktop publishing software, and today you can use Word not only to type text, but to add graphical elements to make a document more engaging for your readers as well.

This chapter starts by showing you how to add shapes using the built-in Word shape editor. Word also allows you to insert pictures and 3D models, either from your own computer or from stock libraries installed with Word. What's more, you can add screenshots on your computer and place screen clippings, which are a portion of your screen, into your document.

Word also contains its own custom diagrams, called SmartArt, so that you can add things like organizational charts and process charts easily.

If you need to add text in an area outside the main area of text, such as in a sidebar, you can add text boxes and modify how the text appears within the text box.

I also talk about formatting your graphics and text boxes, adding text to graphic elements, and positioning those images so that they look good on the page. Finally, you learn how to add alternative, or Alt, text to illustrations and photos so that people who cannot see them can read a description.

Inserting Illustrations and Text Boxes

Word makes it easy to choose and insert shapes, pictures, 3D models, SmartArt graphics, screenshots, screen clippings, and even text boxes all from one location: the Insert menu ribbon. (If the Word window isn't very wide, you may need to click Illustrations in the Ribbon to view a drop-down ribbon that contains many of the icons discussed in this section.)

Adding Shapes

Word contains many built-in *shapes* that you can add to your document, from lines to callouts like the speech balloons you find in graphic novels and comic strips. When you add a shape, you place the item on the page and then size the shape to your needs.

Add a shape by following these steps:

1. Click the Insert menu option.
2. In the Insert ribbon, click Shapes in the Illustrations section.
3. Click a shape icon in the drop-down list (see Figure 5.1). The mouse pointer changes from an arrow to a cross.

FIGURE 5.1   The shapes drop-down list

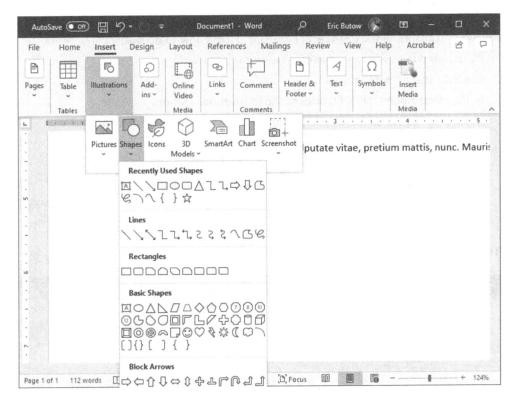

4.   Move the pointer to the location in your document where you want to add the shape.

5.   Hold down the mouse button, and then drag the shape to the size you want.

6.   When you're done, release the mouse button. The shape appears in front of the text in the document.

You'll learn how to wrap text around your image later in this chapter.

   You can also create a separate area for drawing within your document by clicking New Drawing Canvas at the bottom of the drop-down list. A new drawing area appears in the canvas box where your cursor is located so that you can select shapes in the Shape Format ribbon and then draw those shapes within the box.

Including Pictures

You can add *pictures* stored on your computer, stock images that were installed with Word, or pictures available on the Office.com website. Here's how to do this:

1. Place your cursor where you want to insert the image.
2. Click the Insert menu option.
3. In the Insert ribbon, click Pictures in the Illustrations section.
4. In the drop-down menu, shown in Figure 5.2, click one of the following options:

    This Device: Click this to browse for and select a photo from your computer.

    Stock Images: Click this to view and open a stock image on your computer.

    Online Pictures: Click this to view and open an image from Office.com.

    > For this example, I'll open a stock image. By default, the Stock Images tab is open in the photos dialog box.

FIGURE 5.2   Pictures drop-down menu

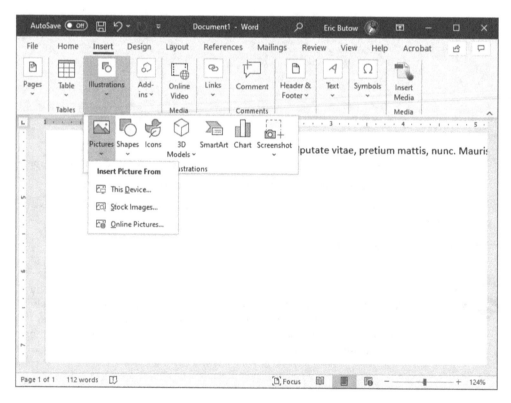

5. Click one of the other tabs to open icons, cut out photos of people, or choose from stickers. I'll keep the default Stock Images.

6. Under the Search box, click one of the category tiles, shown in Figure 5.3, to view photos within that category. You can view more categories by clicking the right arrow at the right side of the category tiles row.

FIGURE 5.3   Category tiles

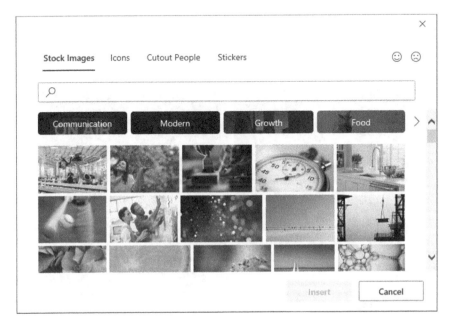

7. Scroll up and down in the list of thumbnail images until you find the one that you want, and then click the image.

8. Click Insert.

The image appears in the document, and text moves underneath the image. You'll learn how to move the image and change the text wrapping style later in this chapter.

Inserting 3D Models

You can insert *3D models* into a document and then change the orientation. Follow these steps:

1. Place your cursor where you want to insert the 3D model.

2. Click the Insert menu option.

3. In the Insert ribbon, click 3D Models in the Illustrations section.

4. You can search for 3D models on your computer or stock 3D models that were installed with Word. For this example, I'll click Stock 3D Models.

5. In the Online 3D Models dialog box (see Figure 5.4), scroll up and down the list of categories and then click the category tile you want.

FIGURE 5.4   3D model category list

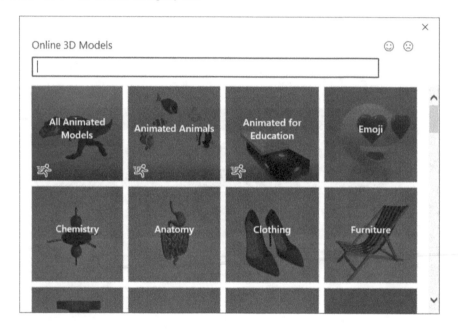

6. Click the 3D model you want and then click Insert.

The model appears in the document in front of the rest of the text. You'll learn how to modify the location and position of the 3D model, as well as change the text wrapping style, later in this chapter.

Adding SmartArt Graphics

SmartArt graphics are built-in art types for conveying specific kinds of information, such as a flow chart to show a process or a decision tree to show a hierarchy. Follow these steps to add a SmartArt graphic:

1. Place your cursor where you want to insert your SmartArt graphic.

2. Click the Insert menu option.

3. In the Insert ribbon, click SmartArt in the Illustrations section.

4. In the Choose A SmartArt Graphic dialog box, shown in Figure 5.5, select a category from the list on the left side of the dialog box.

FIGURE 5.5   SmartArt categories

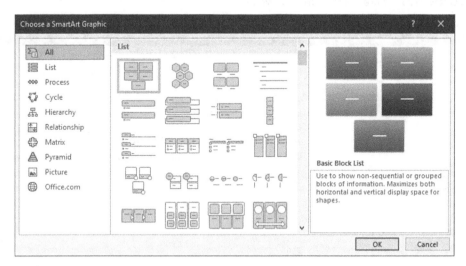

The default is All, which shows all the SmartArt graphics from which you can choose. The list of SmartArt graphic type icons in the center of the dialog box depends on the category you chose. For this example, I chose Hierarchy.

5. Click the graphic type that you want to insert. A description of the graphic type appears at the right side of the dialog box.

6. Click OK.

The graphic appears in the document, and text moves underneath the image.

You'll learn how to set up a graphic to look the way you want, as well as change the text wrapping style, later in this chapter.

Placing Screenshots and Screen Clippings

You can take a photo of another window and add it directly into your document from within Word. You can also clip a portion of your screen within Word and add it to your document automatically.

Screenshot

Add a *screenshot* to your document by following these steps:

1. Place your cursor where you want to insert the screenshot.

2. Click the Insert menu option.

3. In the Insert ribbon, click Screenshot in the Illustrations section. If there are any windows open, Word scans your computer and places thumbnail images of the windows within the drop-down list, as shown in Figure 5.6.

FIGURE 5.6   Screenshots drop-down list

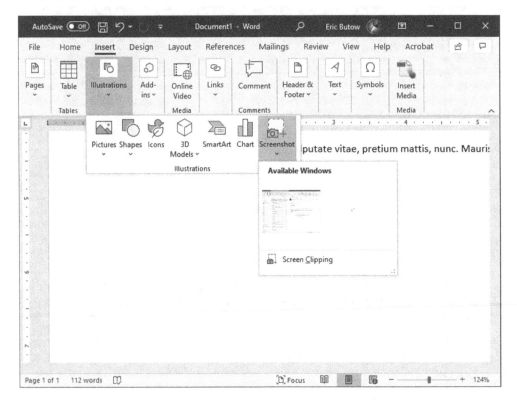

The currently open Word window is one of the windows that Word finds. When you click the window in the list, Word places the screenshot at the insertion point in your document.

Screen Clipping

Here's how to add a *screen clipping*, where you can clip the entire screen or a portion of it:

1. Click Screen Clipping in the drop-down list. Word automatically opens the last window that you had open prior to using Word. If you didn't have a window open, you see the desktop. The screen has a transparent white overlay, and the mouse pointer changes to a cross, which means that Word is ready for you to capture the screen.

2. Move the cursor to the location where you want to start capturing the screen.

3. Hold down the mouse button and drag until you've captured your selection (see Figure 5.7).

4. Release the mouse button.

FIGURE 5.7   Capture area

The clipped image appears under the insertion point in your document and shows Alt text—alternative descriptive text that Word thinks is close to what's in the image, intended for people who can't see the image. You'll learn how to change the Alt text and modify the image later in this chapter.

Inserting Text Boxes

If you want to have an area outside of the text of your document with its own formatting, such as a sidebar, Word allows you to create a separate area of text outside the main area in your document. Then you can place *text boxes* to the side of the text or even over the text. Here's how to add a text box:

1. Place your cursor where you want to insert the text box.

2. Click the Insert menu option.

3. In the Insert ribbon, click Text Box in the Text section. (If the Word window isn't very wide, you may need to click the Text icon in the ribbon to view the Text Box icon in the drop-down ribbon.)

4. In the drop-down list, scroll up and down to view the different text box styles in each thumbnail-sized icon (see Figure 5.8).

FIGURE 5.8   Text box styles

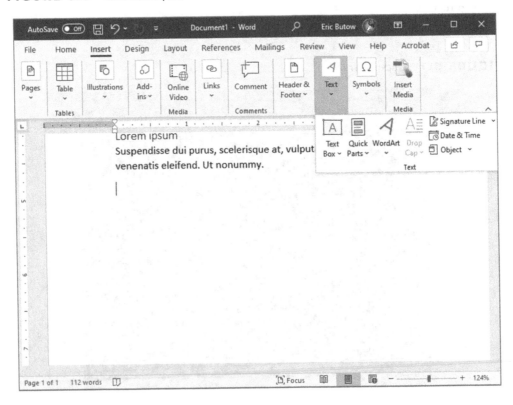

The text box appears at a location near the insertion point, depending on the box you selected, and the style name appears underneath the icon.

You can also view more text boxes, if any, on Office.com by moving the mouse pointer over More Text Boxes From Office.com and then clicking a text box style on the side menu.

You'll learn how to format a text box in the next section.

Draw your own text box by clicking Draw Text Box at the bottom of the drop-down list. When you do, the mouse pointer changes to a cross and you can add a text box on the page by holding down the mouse pointer and dragging the box until it's the size that you want.

After you release the mouse button, the text box appears on the page with a white background and in front of any text. The cursor blinks in the text box so that you can start typing text in the Word default font.

Inserting Shapes and Graphics

1. Go to the page where you want to add a shape or create a new page.

2. Add a pentagon on the page.

3. Go to another page in your document or add a new page.

4. Place your cursor where you want to add a picture.

5. Add a stock image of your choice on the screen.

6. Under the picture, add a 3D model of your choice.

7. Go to another page in your document or add a new page.

8. Place your cursor where you want to add a SmartArt graphic.

9. Add a SmartArt pyramid image of your choice on the screen.

10. Under the SmartArt image, add a new text box and add text within it.

Formatting Illustrations and Text Boxes

After you add an illustration and/or a text box, Word gives you plenty of tools to format them to make them look the way you want and then place them where you want on the page.

Applying Artistic Effects

Word contains 22 *artistic effects* that you can apply to a photo in your document, from making the photo look as if it was drawn with a marker to applying a glow effect. Apply an artistic effect as follows:

1. Click the image.

2. Click the Picture Format menu option.

3. Click Artistic Effects in the Adjust area.

4. Select from the effects by clicking on the effect tile in the drop-down menu (see Figure 5.9). When you place the mouse pointer over the tile for a couple of seconds, the description of the effect appears in a pop-up box.

FIGURE 5.9   The effects tiles

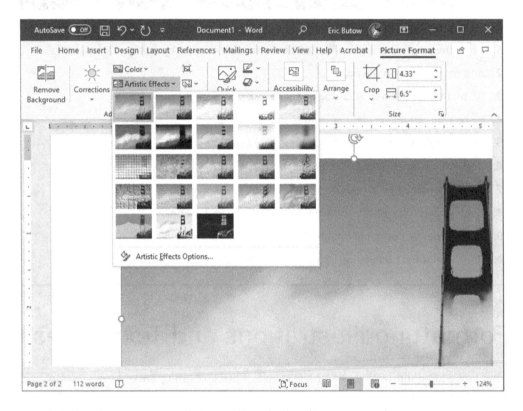

5.   Click the tile you want, and Word will apply the effect to your photo.

Since the effects tiles in the drop-down menu can be small, applying an effect can show you what it looks like. You can always remove the effect once you've seen it by pressing Ctrl+Z.

 You can apply only one artistic effect at a time to a picture. So, applying a different artistic effect removes the previously applied artistic effect.

Adding Picture Effects and Picture Styles

Word also allows you to set effects from within the Picture Format ribbon. However, if you don't need to have fine-tuned effects on your picture, Word has prebuilt styles for you that you can apply to the selected picture by clicking the appropriate tile in the ribbon.

Add a Picture Effect

Here's how to choose and add a *picture effect*:

1. Click the picture.

2. Click the Picture Format menu option.

3. Click Picture Effects in the Picture Styles section.

4. In the drop-down menu, move the mouse pointer to one of the seven effects that you want to add. I selected Shadow in this example.

5. In the side menu, move the mouse pointer over the tile that contains the shadow style. The style is applied to the picture in your document so that you can see what it looks like (see Figure 5.10).

FIGURE 5.10   Offset: Center shadow style applied to the picture

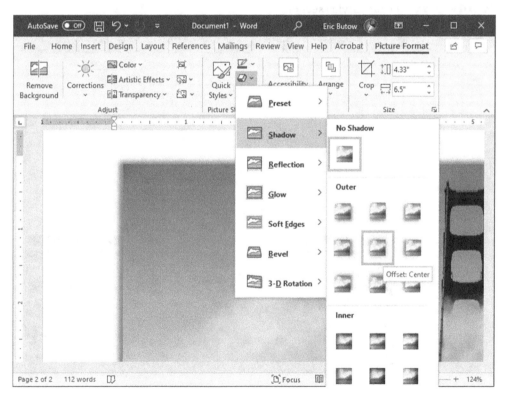

6. When you find an effect that you like, click the tile in the menu.

If you want to change the effect, click Options at the bottom of the menu. For example, in Shadow, click Shadow Options. The Format Picture pane appears on the right side of the Word window so that you can make more detailed changes, such as the color of the shadow.

Apply a Picture Style

Apply a *picture style* from the ribbon by following these steps:

1. Click the image.
2. Click the Picture Format menu option.
3. Move the mouse pointer over the style thumbnail icon in the Picture Styles section, as shown in Figure 5.11. (If the Word window isn't very wide, you may need to click Quick Styles in the ribbon to view a drop-down ribbon with the style icons.)

FIGURE 5.11   Picture Styles section

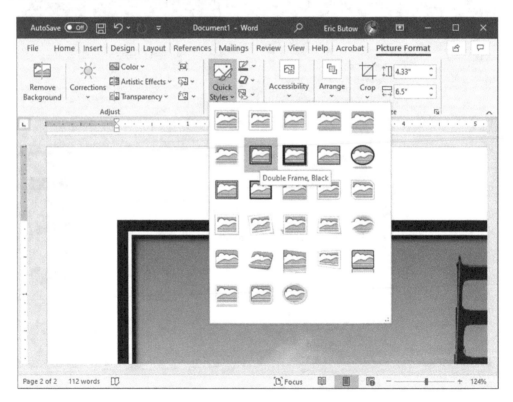

As you move the pointer over every style icon, the picture in your document changes to reflect the style.

4. Apply the style by clicking the icon.

If you don't like any of the styles, move the icon away from the row of styles and the picture reverts to its default state.

Removing Picture Backgrounds

If you want the background of an image to have the background color of the page, here's what to do:

1. Click the image.

2. Click the Picture Format menu option.

3. Click Remove Background at the left side of the ribbon.

   The default background area has the color that Word uses to mark it for removal, whereas the foreground retains its natural coloring (see Figure 5.12).

FIGURE 5.12   Removed background

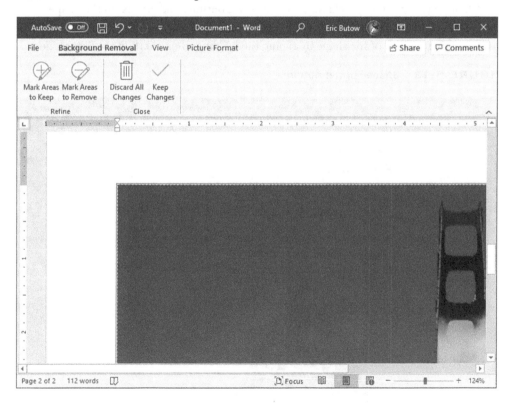

If parts of the picture that you want to keep are magenta (marked for removal), select Mark Areas To Keep and use the free-form drawing pencil to mark the areas on the picture that you want to keep.

To remove more parts of the picture, select Mark Areas To Remove and use the drawing pencil to draw the boundaries of photo areas that you want to remove.

When you're done, select Keep Changes or Discard All Changes.

Formatting Graphic Elements

How you format graphic elements is different depending on the type of graphic you're editing. This section looks at formatting options that you can use aside from the ones detailed previously. In the case of SmartArt, you'll learn more about that in the next section.

Shapes

After you create a shape, the Shape Format menu ribbon appears (see Figure 5.13) so that you can make a variety of changes to the shape, including the following:

- Editing points in the shape by clicking Edit Shape in the Insert Shapes section
- Changing shape styles, including the shape fill, outline, and effects, in the Shape Style section
- Changing the size of the shape by typing the height and/or width in the Size section

FIGURE 5.13   Shape Format ribbon

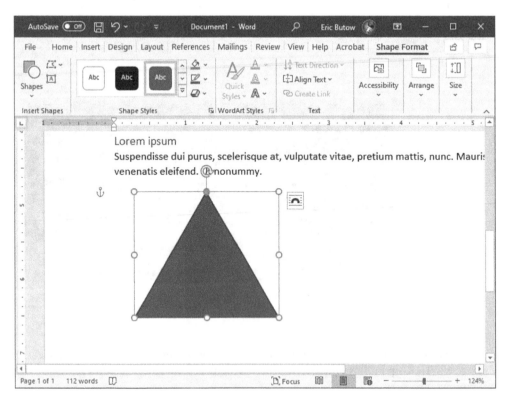

Pictures

In addition to removing picture backgrounds, applying styles, and applying effects, you can format the picture by clicking the Picture Format menu option. In the Picture Format ribbon, shown in Figure 5.14, you can format the picture in various ways:

- Setting corrections (such as brightness and contrast), color, and transparency, setting picture file compression to save disk space, and resetting the picture to its original state in the Adjust section

- Changing the picture border, as well as applying a picture layout style, such as formatting the picture with rounded corners and text underneath, in the Picture Styles section

- Changing the size of the picture by typing the height and/or width in the Size section

FIGURE 5.14   Picture Format ribbon

Screenshots and Screen Clippings

When you add a screenshot or a screen clipping, the Picture Format menu ribbon appears (see Figure 5.15) so that you can make a variety of changes to the shape, including the following:

- Editing points in the shape by clicking Edit Shape in the Insert Shapes section

- Setting shape styles, including the shape fill, outline, and effects, in the Shape Style section

- Changing the size of the shape by typing the height and/or width in the Size section

FIGURE 5.15   Picture Format ribbon

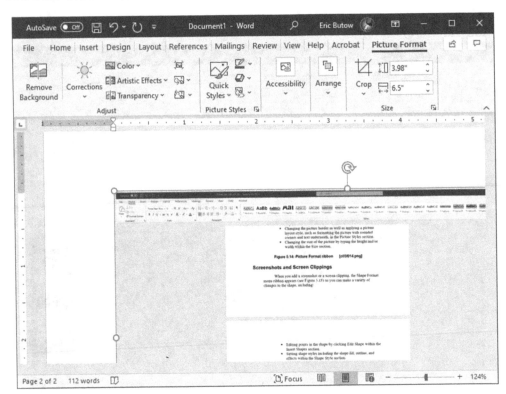

Setting Up SmartArt Graphics

After you add SmartArt, the Type Your Text Here box appears to the left of the image. You can type the text that will appear in the image by clicking [Text] in each bullet line and replacing that template text with your own.

Click the SmartArt Design menu option so that you can make any changes you want in the ribbon. The type of SmartArt you added determines the options that appear in the ribbon.

For example, I created an organizational chart, shown in Figure 5.16, and in the ribbon I can change the following:

- The layout of the chart in the Create Graphic section
- The layout type in the Layouts section
- The chart box colors and styles in the SmartArt Styles section

FIGURE 5.16   Designing an organizational chart using SmartArt

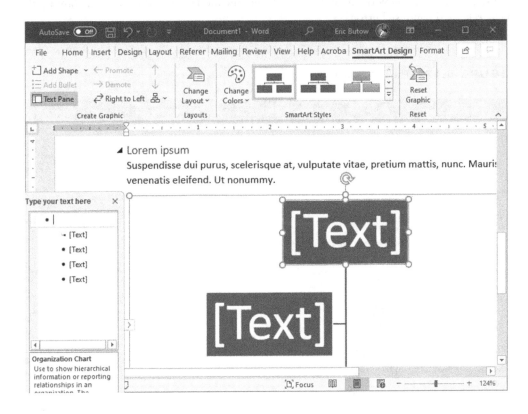

Remove all graphic style changes you made and return the graphic to its original style by clicking the Reset Graphic icon.

When you finish making any changes to your SmartArt graphic, click on the page outside the graphic to deselect it.

Once you stop editing your SmartArt graphic and deselect it, you won't be able to remove any previous changes that you made to the graphic.

Working with 3D Models

You can change the size of a 3D model by clicking the model, clicking one of the circular handles on the perimeter of the selection box, holding down the mouse button, and then dragging. When the model is the size you want, release the mouse button.

Rotate the 3D model 360 degrees in any direction by clicking and holding down the Rotate icon in the middle of the model graphic (see Figure 5.17), and then dragging the mouse pointer to see how the model moves. When the model looks the way you want on the page, release the mouse button.

FIGURE 5.17 The Rotate icon

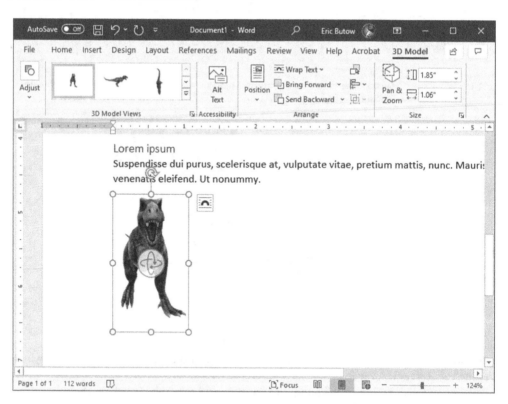

You can change the size of a shape, picture, SmartArt, screenshot, or screen clipping image by clicking the image, moving the mouse pointer over one of the circular handles on the perimeter of the image, holding down the mouse button, and dragging the image. When the image is the size you want, release the mouse button.

EXERCISE 5.2

Formatting Pictures and Graphics

1. Place the cursor in your document where you want to add a picture.

2. Add a stock image of your choice.

3. Select the picture, and then apply the Glow Edges artistic effect.

4. Add another stock image picture in another location in your document.

5. Remove the picture background.

6. Place the cursor in another location in your document.

7. Add a SmartArt pyramid graphic.

8. Switch the layout to an inverted pyramid and apply the Polished style.

9. Add a new 3D model of your choice below the SmartArt graphic.

10. Rotate the model until it looks the way that you want.

Adding and Organizing Text

Word makes it easy to add text, not only in text boxes, but also to your shapes and Smart-Art graphics. What's more, you can format the text to your liking with built-in text styles and alignment options.

Formatting Text in Text Boxes

You can format text in a text box just as you would in the rest of your document. Just click the Home menu option and change the font, paragraph, and styles as you see fit.

You can also format the text in other ways. Select the text that you want to format. Now you can change the text as follows in the Shape Format ribbon.

Apply WordArt Styles

In the WordArt Styles section, you can click one of the three built-in text effect icons (see Figure 5.18):

- Click Text Fill (the letter A on top of a black line) to change the text color in the drop-down menu.

- Click Text Outline (an outlined letter A on top of a black line) to add an outline, including color and outline line width, in the drop-down menu.

- Click Text Effects (a blue outlined letter A) to view and add other effects to the text. In the drop-down menu, move the mouse pointer over one of the effects to see how each effect appears in your photo. You can choose from Shadow, Reflection, Glow, Bevel, 3-D Rotation, or Transform.

FIGURE 5.18   Text effects options in the WordArt Styles section

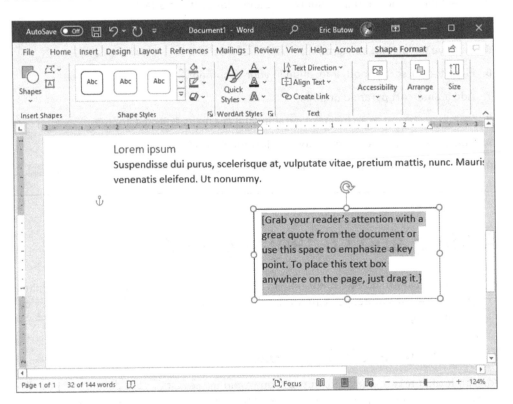

Change Text Appearance

In the Text section, shown in Figure 5.19, you can do three things:

- Click Text Direction to rotate the text 90 degrees or 270 degrees.
- Click Text Alignment to align the text vertically with the top, middle, or bottom of the shape. The default is Middle.
- Click Create Link to link the text to a second text box. When you type so much text in the shape that the shape can't hold any more, the overflow text appears in the second text box.

FIGURE 5.19   Text appearance options in the Text section

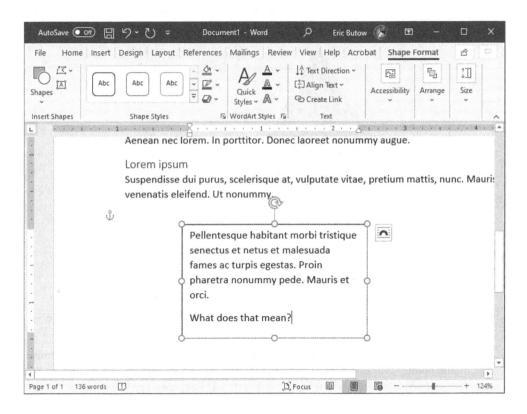

Adding Text in Shapes

When you need to add text in a shape, Word has you covered. Start by right-clicking anywhere in your shape and then clicking Add Text in the context menu.

The cursor appears in the center of the shape so that you can type your text. If you want to format it, select the text that you want to format. Now you can change the style of the text in two sections in the Shape Format ribbon: the WordArt Styles section and the Text section (see Figure 5.20).

FIGURE 5.20 Shape Format ribbon

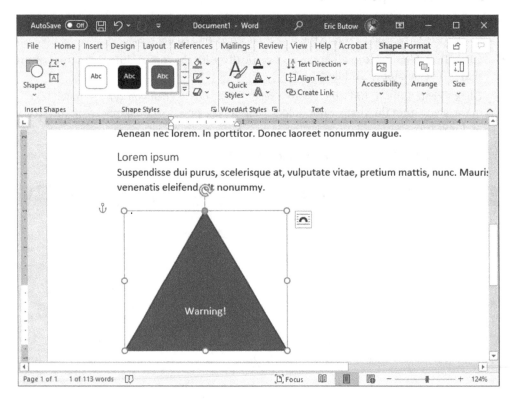

Apply WordArt Styles

In the WordArt Styles section, you can click one of three built-in text effects:

- Click Text Fill to change the text color in the drop-down menu.
- Click Text Outline to add an outline, including color and outline line width, in the drop-down menu.
- Click Text Effects to view and add other effects to the text. In the drop-down menu, move the mouse pointer over one of the effects to see how each effect appears in your photo. You can choose from Shadow, Reflection, Glow, Bevel, 3-D Rotation, and Transform.

Change Text Appearance

In the Text section, you can change the text appearance in one of three ways:

- Click Text Direction to rotate the text 90 degrees or 270 degrees.
- Click Text Alignment to align the text vertically with the top, middle, or bottom of the shape. The default is Middle.
- Click Create Link to link the text to a second text box. When you type so much text in the shape that the shape can't hold any more, the overflow text appears in the second text box.

You can also select the text and use the standard Font, Paragraph, and Styles tools on the Home tab to format your text. You can also right-click your text and change styles in the context menu.

Changing SmartArt Graphic Content

SmartArt graphics include text placeholders automatically. For example, when you create an organizational chart, Word puts text placeholders in each box so that you can fill in those boxes with the appropriate person.

All you have to do is click [Text] in one of the boxes (see Figure 5.21) and then enter your text.

The Type Your Text Here box appears to the left of the graphic. As you enter text in the box, the text appears in the outline in the box. You can add more text by clicking [Text] in each box or by clicking [Text] in each bullet in the outline and typing the text to replace the [Text] placeholder.

FIGURE 5.21   Text in an organizational chart

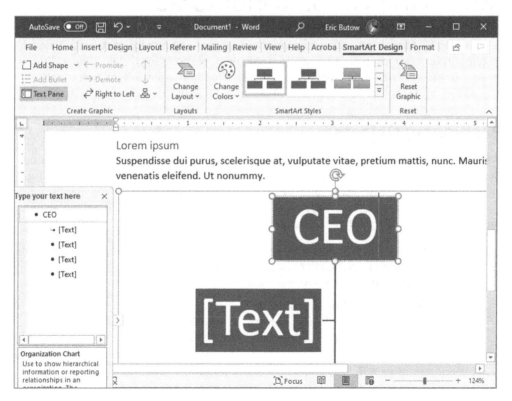

EXERCISE 5.3

Adding Text to Shapes and Graphics

1. Place your cursor on a page where you want to add a shape or create a new page.

2. Add a new shape of your choice.

3. Add text to your shape.

4. Add a new text box underneath the shape.

5. Type text in the text box.

6. Align the text to the top of the text box.

7. Under the text box, add a SmartArt graphic of your choice.

8. Add as much text as you can fit in each entry in the graphic.

Modifying Graphic Elements

Fortunately, Word makes it easy to change where you can put a shape, picture, 3D model, screenshot, or screen clipping (or even all five if you have room) in your document. You can move your objects around on a page and then tell Word how you want the text to move around the image. You can even instruct Word to put text in front of or behind the image.

Positioning Objects

When you add a new shape or image, the image appears in front of the rest of the text on the page, if any. Now you can move the shape or image in your document by moving the mouse pointer over the image, holding down the mouse button, and then moving the image.

If you need to position your shape or image at just the right location, Word gives you three options for moving a shape or image, depending on what you need.

Small Increments If you only need to move your shape or image in small increments to get the position just right, click the picture. Next, hold down the Ctrl key and then click one of the arrow keys to move the image.

Move Several Objects You can move several images or shapes by grouping them together. Start by selecting the first object, and then hold down the Ctrl key. Next, select the other images and/or shapes you want to group.

Now right-click on one of the selected shapes and/or images, move the mouse pointer over Group in the context menu, and then click Group in the side menu. Now you can move all the images and/or shapes around at once.

You can ungroup them by right-clicking one of the images and/or shapes, moving the mouse pointer over Group in the context menu, and then clicking Ungroup in the side menu.

Size and Position   You can specify exact measurements for the size and position of an image, shape, or group by right-clicking the object and then clicking Size and Position in the menu. In the Layout dialog box, you can change size, position, and text wrapping options, which you will learn about in the next section.

Wrapping Text Around Objects

If you want to push text around an image or shape, select the object and then click the Layout Options button to the upper right of the shape. (It looks like an upside-down U.) The Layout Options menu appears and displays icons with the various text wrap options, as shown in Figure 5.22.

FIGURE 5.22   Layout Options menu

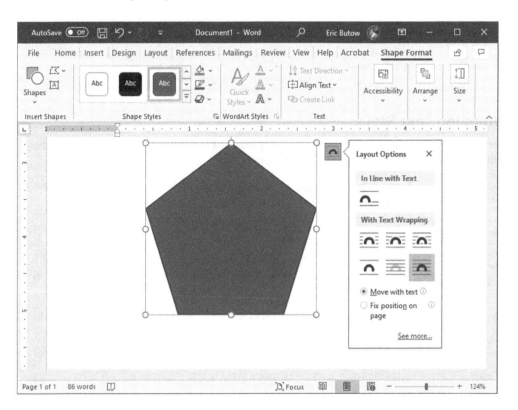

However, this menu doesn't give you as much control as you may need. You can view and change more options by clicking the See More link at the bottom of the menu.

The Layout dialog box appears. If the Text Wrapping tab isn't selected, click it to display the text wrapping options, as shown in Figure 5.23.

FIGURE 5.23   Text Wrapping tab in Layout dialog box

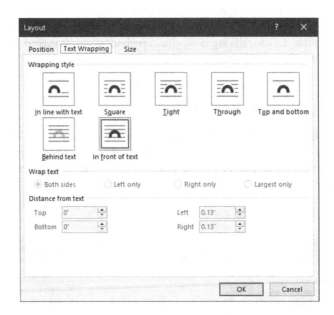

Wrapping Text Styles

The current wrapping text style icon is already selected for you. You can click one of the following seven icons to change the text wrapping style:

In Line With Text   This style places the image or shape in a paragraph just as with any line of text. The picture or shape moves with the paragraph when you add or remove text. As with text, you can cut the image or shape and paste it on another line of text.

Square   This style wraps text around the image or shape in a square pattern. If the image or shape tapers, such as a triangle, then you have white text around the tapered parts of the image or shape.

Tight   The text wraps at the same distance between the edge of the image or shape and the text.

Through   This style allows you to customize the areas in which the text wraps around the visible image, but not any space (either white or a solid color) that surrounds the image. Note that this option does not work with vector images.

Through acts much like Tight, except that you can change the wrap points so that text can fill in the spaces between elements in an image. If the image or shape doesn't have any spaces, then text wrapping works just like Tight.

Top And Bottom   The text wraps on the top and bottom of the image or shape and doesn't put any text along the left or right sides of the photo no matter how wide the image or shape is.

Behind Text   Word places the image or shape behind the text and doesn't wrap the text around it. Note that selecting this option means that you must be more precise when selecting the image or shape with your cursor, because otherwise Word will think you're trying to select the text.

In Front Of Text   Word places the picture or shape on top of the text and doesn't wrap the text. Some of your text may be hidden behind the image or shape, which means some of it may be blocked, depending on the transparency of the image.

These options control whether text wraps around an image on both sides, left, right, or wherever the largest distance between the image and the margin.

Specific Wrapping

The Square, Tight, and Through wrapping styles allow you to add specific distance measurements between text and your image or shape. When you click one of these styles, the Wrap Text and Distance From The Text settings become active.

Both Sides   Wraps text around both sides of the image or shape

Left   Wraps text around only the left side of the image or shape and leaves the space to the right of the image or shape blank

Right   Wraps text around only the right side of the image or shape and leaves the space to the left of the image or shape blank

Largest Only   Wraps text on the side of the image or shape that has the larger distance from the margin. For example, if the distance between the left margin and the image is one inch, and the distance between the image and right margin is 3 inches, Word wraps the text around the right side of the image.

Distance From The Text   You can enter the specific distance between the text and the image or shape in inches. You can independently set distances for the top, bottom, left, and right margins. Also, you can specify the distance in hundredths of an inch if you want to be that precise.

🌐 **Real World Scenario**

Placing Your Graphics for Easy Reading

Your boss has come to you and asked you to put together a document for the sales team. The document is all about the neat new company widget that was just announced, so the boss wants a lot of graphics.

There is a limit to the number of graphics that you should add to a document so as not to overwhelm the reader. A reader's eyes follow a pattern as they look across a page: from the upper-left corner to the lower-right corner, and then to the lower-left corner.

So, if you want to get the attention of your customers (and please your boss), position your graphics in one or more of those locations in your document and then set text wrap settings accordingly. When readers visually scan those graphics, they will likely pick up on some of the text you have in your document, too.

Adding Alt Text to Objects

Alt text, or alternative text, tells anyone who views your document in Word what the image, shape, or SmartArt graphic is when the reader moves their mouse pointer over it. If the reader can't see your document, then Word will use text-to-speech in Windows to read your Alt text to the reader audibly.

Here's how to add Alt text:

1. Click the shape, picture, or SmartArt graphic. If you clicked a SmartArt graphic, skip to step 3.

2. In the Shape Format or Picture Format ribbon, click the Alt Text icon. (If your Word window isn't very wide, you may need to click the Accessibility icon and then click Alt Text.)

3. In the Alt Text pane on the right side of the Word window (see Figure 5.24), type one or two sentences in the text box to describe the object and its context.

   Some images, especially stock images, already have this information in the text box, but you can change it.

4. Click the Mark As Decorative check box if your image, shape, or SmartArt graphic adds visual interest but isn't informative, such as a line.

5. When you're done, close the pane.

FIGURE 5.24   Alt Text pane

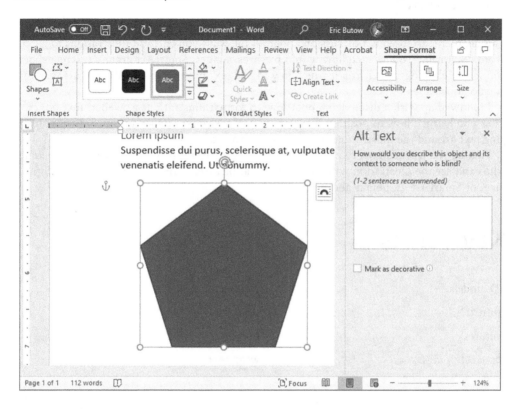

EXERCISE 5.4

Positioning Graphics and Adding Alt Text

1. Place your cursor on a page where you want to add a shape or create a new page.

2. Add a new shape of your choice.

3. Position the shape so that it's on the left side of the page.

4. Wrap text so that it goes around the right of your shape.

5. Add Alt text that describes your shape.

Summary

This chapter started with a discussion about all the ways you can add illustrations to a Word document. You learned how to add pictures, shapes, SmartArt graphics, screenshots, and screen clippings. Then you learned how to add text boxes to have different areas of text in a document.

I followed up with a discussion about how to format illustrations as well as text boxes. Then you learned how to position illustrations and text boxes on a page, including wrapping text around the illustration or text box the way you want.

Finally, you learned how to add Alt text to any type of illustration to ensure that people who can't see the illustration will know what that picture, shape, screenshot, screen clipping, or SmartArt graphic is about.

Key Terms

3D models

Alt text

pictures

screen clippings

screenshots

shapes

text box

wrap text

Exam Essentials

Understand how to add different types of graphics.   Word allows you to add a variety of graphics and photos to your document, including shapes, 3D models, and Word SmartArt graphics. You need to know how to add these graphics as well as pictures, screenshots of open windows, and clip portions of your screen to your document.

Know how to add and format text boxes.   Understand how to add a text box that is separate from other text on a page, modify a text box, and format text in a text box.

Understand how to position graphics and wrap text around them.   Know how to position your graphic on the page and set options for wrapping text around the graphic, moving the text in front of the graphic or moving the graphic in front of the text.

Be able to add Alt text.   Understand why Alt text is important for your readers and know how to add Alt text to a graphic or picture.

Review Questions

1. How do you add a rectangle?

   A. Click the Design menu option, and then select a new theme in the Design ribbon.

   B. Click the Insert menu, and then click SmartArt in the Insert ribbon.

   C. Click the Insert menu option, and then click Shapes in the Insert ribbon.

   D. Select the rectangle style from the Home ribbon.

2. How do you add an organizational chart to your document using the Insert menu ribbon?

   A. Click Shapes.

   B. Click SmartArt.

   C. Click Chart.

   D. Click Pictures.

3. Why should you add a text box?

   A. Because it's easier to read

   B. Because you need to add one before you can start typing text in your document

   C. You don't need to add one because you can add text directly on a page.

   D. To have text separate from the rest of the text in your document

4. How do you apply a specific picture style in the Picture Format ribbon?

   A. Click the Corrections icon.

   B. Click one of the picture styles tiles in the Picture Styles area.

   C. Click Picture Effects.

   D. Click Change Picture.

5. How do you clear style changes that you made to a SmartArt graphic?

   A. Use the SmartArt Design menu ribbon.

   B. Delete the SmartArt graphic.

   C. Click the Undo icon in the title bar.

   D. Use the Format menu ribbon.

6. How do you rotate a selected 3D model?

   A. Click one of the icons in the 3D Model Views section in the 3D Model menu ribbon.

   B. Click and drag the handles on the selection box around the model.

   C. Click and drag the icon in the middle of the model.

   D. Click the Position icon in the 3D Model menu ribbon.

7. If you have two text boxes in your document, how can you link them together?

    A. Click the Insert menu option, and then click Link in the ribbon.

    B. Use the Shape Format menu ribbon.

    C. Use the Layout ribbon.

    D. Click the Sort icon on the Home ribbon.

8. How do you add text to a shape?

    A. Use the Shape Format ribbon.

    B. Click the Layout Option icon next to the selected shape.

    C. Use the Insert ribbon.

    D. Right-click the shape.

9. How do you place a graphic so that it remains with the text above and below it when you wrap the text?

    A. Top and bottom

    B. Both sides

    C. In line with text

    D. Square

10. Why should you add Alt text to graphics and pictures?

    A. Because it's required for all graphics in a Word document

    B. To help people who can't see the graphic know what the graphic is about

    C. Because Word won't save your document until you do

    D. Because you want to be as informative as possible

Chapter

6

Working with Other Users on Your Document

MICROSOFT EXAM OBJECTIVES COVERED IN THIS CHAPTER:

✓ **Manage document collaboration**

- Add and manage comments

  - Add comments

  - Review and reply to comments

  - Resolve comments

  - Delete comments

- Manage change tracking

  - Track Changes

  - Review tracked changes

  - Accept and reject tracked changes

  - Lock and unlock change tracking

Word is built for sharing documents with others, which is vital whether you work with several people in one office or people in more than one location. Microsoft includes a tool in Word that allows you to add *comments*, which appear within boxes in the right margin of the page. This approach ensures that the comments don't clutter or obscure the page text. You can also reply to comments within a comments box. If you are the person who sends a document for review and are responsible for managing all of the comments, Word also includes tools for resolving comments and deleting them as well.

If other people will be adding information directly in the document, Word has a nifty *Track Changes* feature that allows you to view all additions and deletions that other reviewers made. You can also decide what level of changes you want to view on the page.

All reviewers can accept and/or reject tracked changes. And, if you don't want people either to turn Track Changes off or accept or reject changes, you can lock Track Changes before you send the document for review.

Adding Comments

It's easy to add a comment about something in your document within the text itself. However, if you use comments in the text, you can clutter up your pages with a lot of comments, even if they are in a different style that sets comment text apart from the rest. Comments in text can also add to your page count, which may throw off reviewers who expect the document to be a set number of pages long.

What to do? Use the Review menu option to add a new comment in a new, right margin that Word creates automatically. These comments appear in a box and point to the place in the text where you added the comment.

Inserting Comments

Here's how to insert a comment into a document:

1. Select the text on which you want to comment.
2. Click the Review menu option.
3. In the Review menu ribbon, click New Comment in the Comments section.

Word shows your comment in a box in a margin appended to the right side of the page (see Figure 6.1).

FIGURE 6.1   A new comment

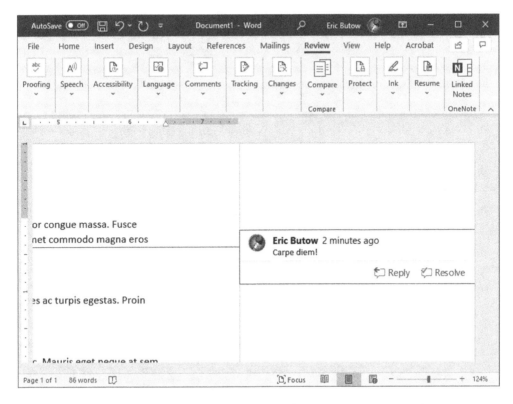

The outline color represents the default color of the primary reviewer. (That's you.) As you type the comment, you can press Enter to break up sections of your comment for easier reading. Word assigns different colors to different commenters automatically.

When you're done, click in the document again. The comment appears in the margin.

At the top of the comment box, Word displays your Microsoft 365 username, your avatar, and how long ago you wrote the comment. An avatar is an icon that you created for yourself when you created a Microsoft 365 account. If you don't have one, then Word shows a placeholder avatar.

Reviewing and Replying to Comments

You can review comments by scrolling through the document, but you can also use the Review menu ribbon to go to the next comment. Start by clicking the Review menu option. In the Review menu ribbon, click Next in the Comments section to see the next comment (see Figure 6.2).

FIGURE 6.2   The next comment

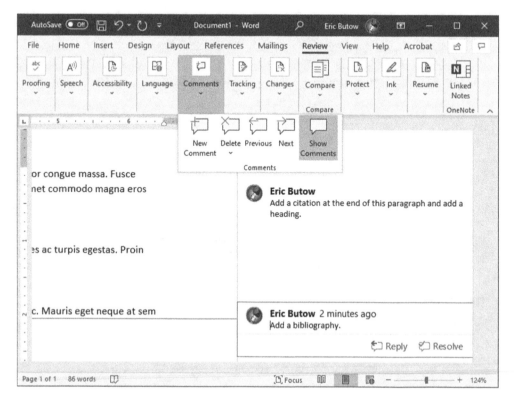

Word takes you to the page that contains the next comment in the document. Go to the previous comment in the document by clicking Previous in the ribbon.

If you see a comment from someone else (or even yourself) and you want to reply, click Reply in the comment box and then enter your reply. When you're finished, click in the document. You see the reply indented underneath the first comment.

Resolving Comments

When you decide that a comment is resolved but you want to keep the comment in the document for your notes or to let reviewers know the comment is resolved, click Resolve in the lower-right corner of the comment box.

The comment text is gray. When you place the cursor in the document, only the commenter name and the first few words in the comment (about 40 characters) appear in the margin, but the comment isn't deleted, as shown in Figure 6.3.

FIGURE 6.3   Resolved comment

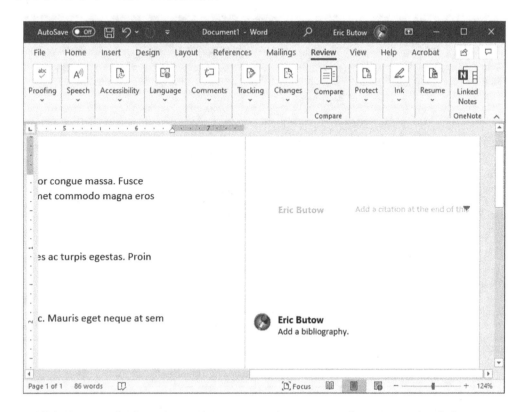

Click the grayed-out comment to view it. You can reopen the comment by clicking Reopen in the lower-right corner of the comment box.

Deleting Comments

Here's how to delete one or more comments when you decide that you no longer need them:

1. Click in the comment box.
2. Click the Review menu option, if necessary.
3. In the Review menu ribbon, click the Delete icon in the Comments section (see Figure 6.4).

Word deletes the comment and any replies within that comment.

FIGURE 6.4   Deleting a comment

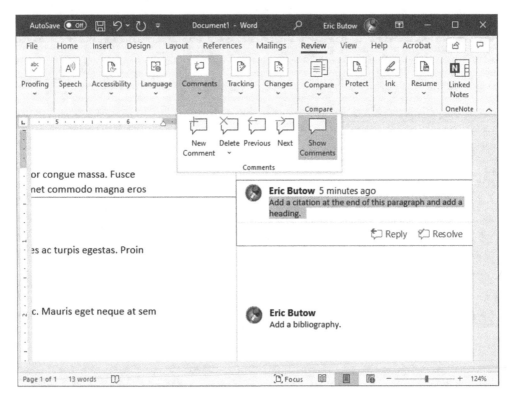

You can delete all comments in the document, even without selecting a comment, by clicking the down arrow underneath the Delete icon in the ribbon. In the drop-down menu, click Delete All Comments. All comments in the document disappear, and so does the appended margin on the right side of the page.

EXERCISE 6.1

Inserting, Replying to, and Deleting a Comment

1. Place your cursor where you want to add a comment in your document.

2. Write a new comment.

3. Reply to your comment.

4. Resolve the comment.

5. Restore the comment you resolved.

6. Delete the comment.

Tracking Your Changes

The Track Changes feature is vital when you review changes made by other reviewers. You can see what changes were made, when they were made, and by whom. When you have Track Changes on, Word alerts you to changes in the text with vertical *change lines* that reflect the reviewer color assigned by Word.

By default, Track Changes only shows change lines, not any other formatting in the text such as strikethrough text for deletions, which Word calls *markup*. You will learn how to display different markup levels later in this chapter.

Turning On Track Changes

Word does not turn on Track Changes automatically when you open a new document, so you have to turn the feature on. Start by clicking the Review menu option. In the Review menu ribbon, click the Track Changes icon in the Tracking section, as shown in Figure 6.5.

FIGURE 6.5   Track Changes icon

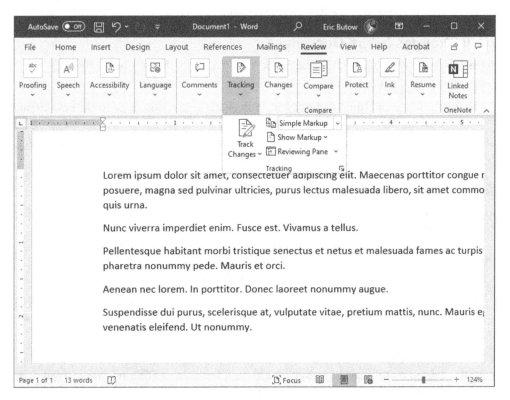

Now the Track Changes icon in the ribbon has a gray background, which means that Track Changes is on. You can turn off Track Changes by following the same steps you took to turn on the feature.

When Track Changes is off, Word stops marking changes. However, the changes in your document remain until you accept or reject them, which you'll learn about later in this chapter.

 If you can't turn on Track Changes, you might need to turn off the document protection feature. In the Protect section in the Review ribbon, click Restrict Editing, and then click Stop Protection in the Restrict Editing panel on the right side of the Word window. You may also need to type the document password to gain access.

Reviewing Tracked Changes

You can review tracked changes by just scrolling through the document, but that can be cumbersome for long documents. Word makes it easy for you to go to the next or previous change in your document in the Review menu ribbon.

View Changes in the Document

Here's how to view changes in the document from within the Review menu ribbon:

1. Click the Review menu option.

2. In the Review menu ribbon, click Next in the Changes section to go to the next change in the document.

3. Click Previous in the Changes section to go to the previous change in the document (see Figure 6.6).

Modify Change Markup Settings

You can also review tracked changes by setting how Word displays changes in the document from within the Review menu ribbon.

In the Tracking section in the ribbon, click the down arrow to the right of Simple Markup (see Figure 6.7).

Next, click one of the four options in the drop-down menu:

Simple Markup: This is the default selection. You see only change lines. All added and deleted text still appears in the document, but without any formatting such as strikethrough text.

All Markup: This is where you see all the change formatting. In addition to change bars, deleted text is marked with strikethrough format and additions are marked with an underline. The text also sports the colors of various reviewers who made changes.

No Markup: This option shows any added text (or doesn't show any deleted text) but does not show any other markup formatting, including change bars.

Original: This means you see the document without any changes that have been made to it.

FIGURE 6.6 Previous and Next options

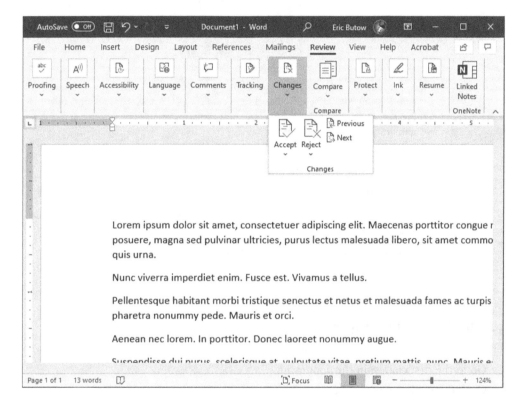

Accepting and Rejecting Tracked Changes

Word gives you the power to accept one change, several changes, or all changes in the document. The same is true for rejecting changes made by other reviewers.

> If you can't see any changes in the text before you accept or reject changes, change the markup setting to All Markup, as described in the previous section.

FIGURE 6.7   Markup drop-down menu

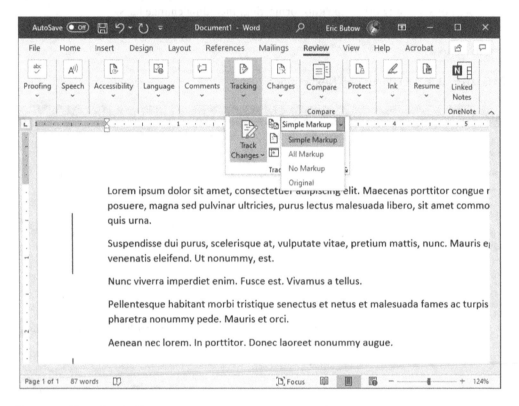

Accept Tracked Changes

Here's how to accept one, several, or all changes:

1. Go to the first change in the document.

2. Click the Review menu option.

3. In the Review menu ribbon, click the down arrow under the Accept icon in the Changes section (see Figure 6.8).

4. In the drop-down menu, click one of the following options:

   - Accept the change by clicking Accept This Change.

   - Accept the change and move to the next one by clicking Accept And Move To Next.

   - Accept all changes in the document, but keep Track Changes on, by clicking Accept All Changes.

   - Accept all changes and turn off Track Changes by clicking Accept All Changes And Stop Tracking.

FIGURE 6.8 Accept menu

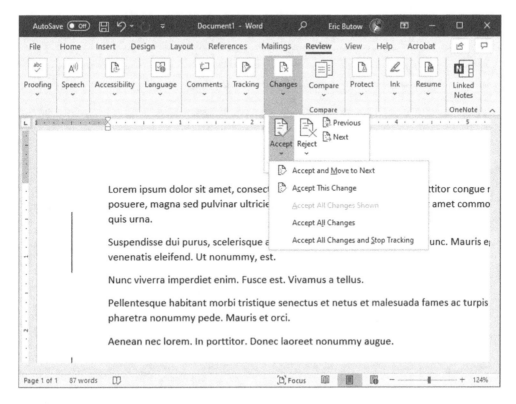

Now you can go to the previous change by clicking Previous in the ribbon or go to the next change by clicking Next.

Reject Tracked Changes

Here's how to reject one, several, or all changes in your document:

1. Go to the change in the document that you want to reject.

2. Click the Review menu option.

3. In the Review menu ribbon, click the down arrow under the Reject icon in the Changes section (see Figure 6.9).

4. In the drop-down menu, click one of the following options:

   - Reject the change by clicking Reject Change. Word removes all the changes.

   - Reject the change and move to the next one by clicking Reject And Move To Next.

   - Reject all changes in the document, but keep Track Changes on, by clicking Reject All Changes.

   - Reject all changes and turn off Track Changes by clicking Reject All Changes And Stop Tracking.

FIGURE 6.9   Reject menu

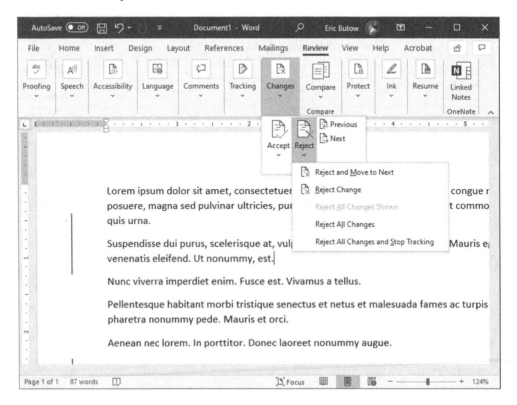

Now you can go to the previous change by clicking Previous in the ribbon or go to the next change by clicking Next.

Locking and Unlocking Change Tracking

If you want to lock Track Changes so that you don't turn the feature off until you have to, or you want your reviewers to know Track Changes should stay on, here's how to do it:

1. Click the Review menu option.

2. In the Review menu ribbon, click the Track Changes text underneath the Track Changes icon in the Tracking section.

3. In the drop-down menu shown in Figure 6.10, click Lock Tracking.

   The Lock Tracking dialog box appears so that you can add a password to keep anyone but yourself from accepting changes, rejecting changes, and turning Track Changes off.

4. Lock changes without adding a password by moving ahead to step 7. Otherwise, continue to step 5.

5. Type your password in the Enter Password (Optional) box.

6. Type the password again in the Reenter To Confirm box.

7. Click OK.

FIGURE 6.10   Track Changes drop-down menu

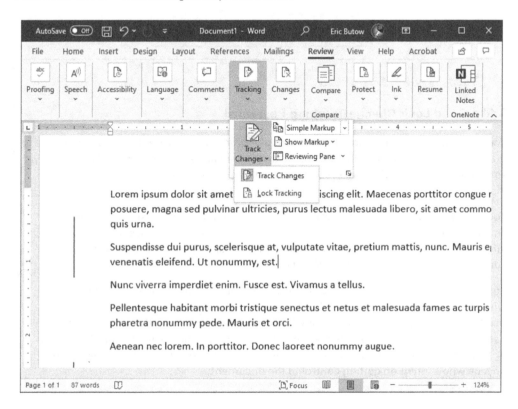

Now the Track Changes icon in the ribbon is disabled, so people can't turn off Track Changes.

You can unlock Track Changes by following steps 1 through 3. If you have no password, then Word unlocks Track Changes.

If you have a password, the Unlock Password dialog box appears (see Figure 6.11). Type the password in the Password box and then click OK.

Once you unlock Track Changes, the ribbon shows that Track Changes is on. You can turn off Track Changes by clicking the Track Changes icon, or by accepting or rejecting all changes and turning off Track Changes, as you learned to do earlier in this chapter.

FIGURE 6.11   Unlock Password dialog box

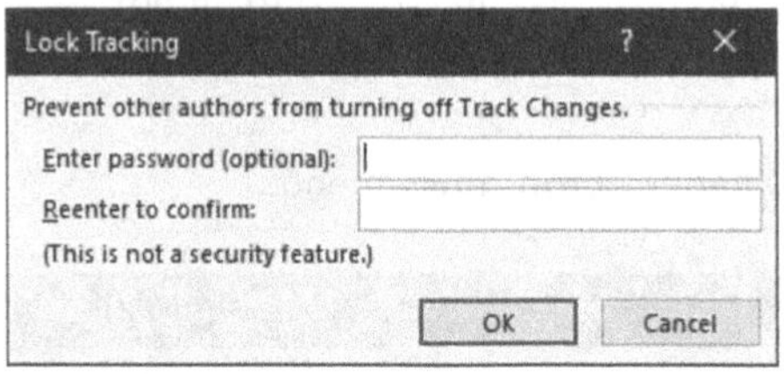

Real World Scenario

Add a Good Lock Change Tracking Password

You're responsible for creating the new product information booklet for the company's brand-new product. This document will be distributed at trade shows around the country, so different people at different offices will need to review the document and comment on it.

You don't know who else in each office will review the document besides the sales and marketing teams. You also don't know most of the people on those teams. The information from the product management team doesn't have all its photos ready yet, so you just need to share the text in a Word document.

You've decided to lock Track Changes to give you control, but anyone can just turn it off when they feel like it. That could add a lot of confusion to the editing process. So, you need to add a password when you lock Track Changes, but be mindful: you need to use a password that you know but one that others can't guess easily. Using the product name or a simple numeric code like 12345 will make it likely that the lock will be bypassed by anyone who's intent on getting control of the document.

EXERCISE 6.2

Track Changes

1. Turn Track Changes on.

2. View All Markup.

3. Add new text and edit existing text in your document so that you can see how Word shows additions and deletions.

4. Accept all changes.

5. Turn off Track Changes.

Summary

This chapter started by showing you how to add comments to a document. Once you learned about adding comments, I discussed how to add a reply to a comment and how to resolve a comment but keep the comment in the document for future reference by you and/ or your reviewers.

You also learned how to use the Review menu ribbon to move between comments in your document, as well as how to delete one or all comments within a document.

Next, I discussed how to turn Track Changes on and off so that you can see which reviewer made changes in which text. You also learned how to change the Track Changes view settings to view certain elements of Track Changes markup text and change lines. Then you learned how to move through all of the changes and accept and reject one or all changes.

I wrapped up the chapter with a discussion about locking Track Changes so that no other users can accept or reject changes or turn off Track Changes.

Key Terms

change lines   markup

comments   track changes

Exam Essentials

Understand how to add and manage comments.   Know how to add a comment to a document, reply to a comment, resolve a comment, restore a comment if the issue is not resolved after all, and delete one or all comments in a document.

Know how to turn on and use Track Changes.   Understand how to turn Track Changes on and off, how to view different types of markup in the document, and how to accept and reject changes.

Be able to lock and unlock Track Changes.   Know why you need to lock Track Changes when you share documents, how to add a password when locking Track Changes, and how to unlock Track Changes.

Review Questions

1. How can you tell who wrote a comment?
    - **A.** The color of the change bar
    - **B.** The color of the box around the comment
    - **C.** The Review menu ribbon tells you who wrote it.
    - **D.** The person's name appears at the top of the comment box.

2. How do you respond directly to a comment?
    - **A.** Click Resolve in the comment box.
    - **B.** Click Reply in the comment box.
    - **C.** Write another comment.
    - **D.** Click the Reject icon in the Review menu ribbon.

3. How do you know a comment is resolved?
    - **A.** The comment no longer appears in the document.
    - **B.** The Show Comments icon in the Review menu ribbon is no longer selected.
    - **C.** The comment is grayed out in the right margin.
    - **D.** Track Changes turns off.

4. How do you restore a resolved comment?
    - **A.** Click the Accept icon in the Review menu ribbon.
    - **B.** Click the comment and then click Reopen.
    - **C.** Create a new comment so that you can repeat your question and/or ask the person who commented to insert their comment again.
    - **D.** Show All Markup.

5. How do you delete all comments in a document?
    - **A.** Click in the comment, and then click the Resolve icon.
    - **B.** Click the Delete icon in the Review menu ribbon.
    - **C.** Click the Reject icon in the Review menu ribbon, and then click Reject All Changes in the menu.
    - **D.** Click the Delete icon in the Review menu ribbon, and then click Delete All Comments in the menu.

6. What menu option do you need to click to open Track Changes?
    - **A.** Review
    - **B.** View
    - **C.** Home
    - **D.** Insert

7. How do you see markup formatting within your document?

  A. Turn on Track Changes.

  B. Select All Markup in the Review menu ribbon.

  C. Click Show Markup in the Review menu ribbon.

  D. Click Accept in the Review menu ribbon.

8. How do you reject every change in your document and keep Track Changes on?

  A. Click Reject in the Review menu ribbon, and then click Reject And Move To Next in the drop-down menu.

  B. Click the Reject icon in the Review menu ribbon.

  C. Click Reject in the Review menu ribbon, and then click Reject All Changes in the drop-down menu.

  D. Show No Markup.

9. How do you accept a change and then move to the preceding change to review it?

  A. Click the Accept icon in the Review menu ribbon.

  B. Click Previous in the Review menu ribbon, and then click the Accept icon.

  C. Click the down arrow under the Accept icon, and then click Accept And Move To Next.

  D. Click the Accept icon, and then click the Previous icon.

10. Why should you add a password when you lock Track Changes?

  A. To keep others from unlocking Track Changes

  B. Because you don't trust other people with whom you share your documents

  C. Because Word requires it

  D. To keep people from turning Track Changes on

Appendix: Answers to Review Questions

Chapter 1: Working with Documents

1. C. Open the Find And Replace dialog box by clicking the Replace icon in the Home ribbon or by pressing Ctrl+H. Then type the existing and replacement text in the Find and Replace fields, respectively. Replace all instances of the existing text by clicking the Replace All button.

2. B. A watermark is lighter background text that conveys the document status to your readers, such as a document that's confidential and only available to certain people to read.

3. D. The header is the area between the top of the page and the top margin.

4. C. The File screen contains the Info menu option so that you can inspect documents.

5. A. When you click in a paragraph in your text and click a style that has the paragraph marker to the right of the name in the Styles list, Word applies all the formatting settings contained within the style to the selected paragraph.

6. D. A theme is a collection of styles for formatting various parts of your page, such as heading text, body text, headers, and footers.

7. B. The Share option gives you several options for sending a document either as an email attachment or on the web in a variety of formats.

8. C. In the Home ribbon, click the down arrow to the right of the Find icon, and then click Go To in the drop-down menu. (You can also press Ctrl+G.)

9. D. The Accessibility Checker inspects your document and checks to see if any potential problems exist that could keep people of different abilities from reading it.

10. B. The Compatibility Checker ensures that your document can be read by three earlier versions of Word dating back to Word 97, and it alerts you to any formatting issues that you may need to change so that all your recipients can read your document.

Chapter 2: Inserting and Formatting Text

1. C. When you click Advanced Find in the Home ribbon, the Find And Replace dialog box appears so that you can change more search options.

2. B. You can open the Find And Replace dialog box by clicking Replace in the Home ribbon and then clicking the Match Case dialog box to specify that the text you want to find has one or more letters in a different case.

3. D. Open the Symbol window from the Insert ribbon by clicking the Symbol icon and then clicking the More Symbols option in the drop-down menu. Then you can add a special character using the Special Characters tab.

4. A. To change the format of multiple selections in your document, you must first double-click Format Painter.

5. C. Word makes it easy to copy the format of a selected block of text by double-clicking the Format Painter icon. Then you can apply it to as much text in the document as you want.

6. D. Word allows you to create a maximum of three columns.

7. B. By default, Word adds a ½-inch indent to the first line of the paragraph, but subsequent lines are not indented.

8. A. Word automatically adds a new page after the one into which you inserted the page break, and you can start typing in the new page.

9. C. After you click Column in the Breaks drop-down menu, a new column appears on the page or on the next page so that you can type more text.

10. B. A section is a portion of the document that has its own formatting on the same page or a new page.

Chapter 3: Managing Tables and Lists

1. C. After you move the mouse pointer over Quick Tables, click the table style that you want to place on the page.

2. B. When you move the mouse pointer over the grid, you can highlight three columns and seven rows and then click the lower-right corner of the highlighted grid to insert the table on the page.

3. C. Sorting from Z to A is descending order. Sorting from A to Z is ascending order.

4. A. Hold down the Alt key as you click and drag on the column so that you can see the exact measurement.

5. D. The built-in AutoFit feature allows you to fit the size of your table or a column automatically to the longest block of content.

6. A. Both the Table Design and Layout menu options appear at the right side of the row of options in the menu bar.

7. B. You can use bullets from symbols, fonts, and even pictures.

8. C. You can sort by text, which is the default search type, as well as by numbers and dates in a table.

9. C. At the beginning of a new paragraph, you can start a bulleted list by pressing the asterisk (*) key, a space, and then some text. Word automatically converts the asterisk to the default bullet style.

10. D. Word gets confused when you update numbers in text and then you try to add a new number in the list. So, use the Numbering feature to keep your lists numbered correctly.

Chapter 4: Building References

1. C. When you click the References menu option, the ribbon shows you options for adding footnotes, endnotes, and more.

2. B. After you select text in the footnote, the pop-up menu appears above the footnote so that you can easily change the font, spacing, and paragraph styles.

3. C. Word automatically applies the correct citation format for the writing style that you need to use for your document, so you don't need to change the format manually.

4. A. After you click Edit Citation in the menu, add the page number in the Edit Citation dialog box and then click OK.

5. D. After you place the cursor where you want to add the placeholder, click Add New Placeholder, type the placeholder name in the Placeholder Name dialog box, and then click OK.

6. A. Word uses its built-in heading styles to determine how many times text with a certain heading style should be indented in the TOC.

7. B. You can open the Styles pane by pressing Alt+Ctrl+Shift+S to view all nine TOC styles based on all the style levels, and then modify each style as you see fit.

8. C. A TOC reflects the layout of your document when you created it, but Word doesn't update the TOC with any other text you added to the document unless you update the TOC manually.

9. C. Word applies the correct formats for your desired writing style into your bibliography, so you don't have to change any formatting manually.

10. D. When you click Bibliography in the References menu ribbon, the three built-in bibliography styles appear in the drop-down menu.

Chapter 5: Adding and Formatting Graphic Elements

1. C. When you click the Insert menu option, click Shapes to view a wide variety of shapes you can add from the drop-down menu.

2. B. When you click the SmartArt icon in the ribbon, the Choose A SmartArt Graphic dialog box opens so that you can select a prebuilt graphic from eight different categories.

3. D. A text box is useful when you want to have text that stands apart from the rest of the text, such as a sidebar, so that you can have additional information on a side of the page that doesn't interfere with the main block of text.

4. C. After you click Picture Effects, you can change an effect in one of the six effect categories.

5. A. In the SmartArt Design menu ribbon, click the Reset Design icon to clear all of your previous changes and return to the original style.

6. C. Clicking and dragging the Rotate button that appears in the middle of the selected model lets you rotate the 3D model.

7. B. After you create at least two text boxes, click in the first one. Then click Create Link in the Text section in the Shape Format menu ribbon. You can then tell Word which text box will receive overflow text.

8. D. After you right-click the shape, select Add Text from the context menu.

9. C. Placing your graphic in line with text means that the graphic is embedded at the insertion point in the text. The text above and below the graphic will stay that way, even as you add more to the document.

10. B. If you're sharing a Word document online with other people in your company who may not be able to see the graphics in your document, then Alt text is a great way to tell those people about the messages in your graphics.

Chapter 6: Working with Other Users on Your Document

1. D. The top of the comment box in the right margin tells you the name of the person who wrote the comment, shows the writer's avatar, and tells you how long ago the person wrote the comment.

2. B. Click Reply in the comment box to write your reply within the comment box.

3. C. The comment and the name of the person who wrote it are grayed out in the right margin of the document, but the comment remains in case you want to reopen it.

4. B. After you click Reopen in the comment box, the comment is restored so that you can add to your comment or reply to it.

5. D. After you click Delete All Comments in the menu, all comments and the right margin in your document disappear.

6. A. The Track Changes option is available in the Review menu ribbon.

7. B. In the Review menu ribbon, click the down arrow to the right of Simple Markup and then click All Markup. You see all of the formatting in the text as well as the change bars in the left margin.

8. C. After you click the Reject icon in the Review menu ribbon, click Reject All Changes. All of the changes made in the document disappear.

9. D. After you accept a change, click the Previous icon to go to the previous change in the document.

10. A. If you want to make sure that people do not turn off Track Changes when they make any changes to a document you've shared, add a password that only you know.

Index

Online Test Bank

Register to gain one year of FREE access after activation to the online interactive test bank to help you study for your Microsoft Office Specialist certification exam for Word—included with your purchase of this book! All of the chapter review questions and the practice tests in this book are included in the online test bank so you can practice in a timed and graded setting.

Register and Access the Online Test Bank

To register your book and get access to the online test bank, follow these steps:

1. Go to bit.ly/SybexTest (this address is case sensitive)!
2. Select your book from the list.
3. Complete the required registration information, including answering the security verification to prove book ownership. You will be emailed a pin code.
4. Follow the directions in the email or go to www.wiley.com/go/sybextestprep.
5. Find your book on that page and click the "Register or Login" link with it. Then enter the pin code you received and click the "Activate PIN" button.
6. On the Create an Account or Login page, enter your username and password, and click Login or, if you don't have an account already, create a new account.
7. At this point, you should be in the test bank site with your new test bank listed at the top of the page. If you do not see it there, please refresh the page or log out and log back in.